101 THINGS® TO DO WITH A
DUTCH OVEN

101 THINGS® TO DO WITH A
DUTCH OVEN

VERNON WINTERTON

Gibbs Smith

Second Edition
28 27 26 25 24 5 4 3 2 1

First Gibbs Smith edition published in 2006
Second Gibbs Smith edition published February 2024

Published by
Gibbs Smith
P.O. Box 667
Layton, Utah 84041

1.800.835.4993 orders
www.gibbs-smith.com

Designed by Ryan Thomann and Renee Bond
Printed and bound in China
Gibbs Smith books are printed on either recycled, 100% post-consumer waste, FSC-certified papers or on paper produced from sustainable PEFC-certified forest/controlled wood source. Learn more at www.pefc.org.

The Library of Congress has cataloged the first edition as follows:

Winterton, Vernon.
101 things to do with a dutch oven / by Vernon Winterton.—1st ed.
p. cm.
ISBN 1-58685-785-1 (first edition)
1. Dutch oven cookery. I. Title: One hundred one things to do with a dutch oven. II. Title.

TX840.D88W56 2006
641.5'89—dc22

ISBN: 978-1-4236-6559-5

This book is dedicated to my mentor, the man who taught me to cook in a Dutch oven, A. Tom Price. Also, to all my friends who I have cooked with and learned from. And especially my wife, Barbara, whose name should follow mine in the byline—she helped me with every recipe.

CONTENTS

Helpful Hints » 8

#1–11 Breakfast

Cinnamon Rolls » 12
Sticky Buns » 13
Apple Dumpling Rolls » 14
Orange Cranberry Rolls » 15
Raisin Bread » 16
Breakfast Rolls » 17
Cinnamon Pull-Aparts » 18
Breakfast Pizza » 19
Royal Braid » 20
Mountain Man Breakfast » 21
Cheesy Breakfast Casserole » 22

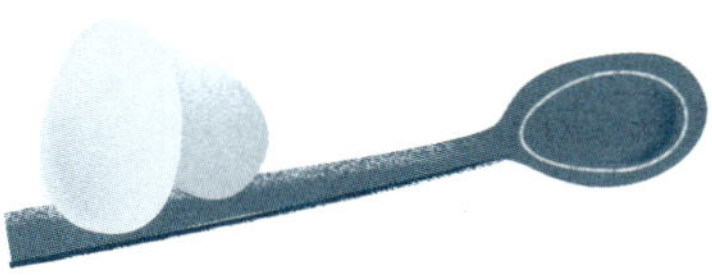

#12–29 Breads & Rolls

Basic White Bread » 24
Potato Bread » 25
Garlic Bread » 26
Easy Onion Soup Bread » 27
Italian Herb and Cheese Loaf » 28
Russian Black Bread » 29
Jalapeño Cheese Bread » 30
One-Bowl Dinner Rolls » 31
Golden Honey Sourdough Rolls » 32
Simple French Bread » 33
Basic Dinner Rolls » 34
Rolls Supreme » 35
Parmesan Herb Twists » 36
Pumpernickel Rolls » 37
Licorice Dill Rolls » 38
Crescent Rolls » 39
Sourdough Starter » 40
Sourdough Bread » 41

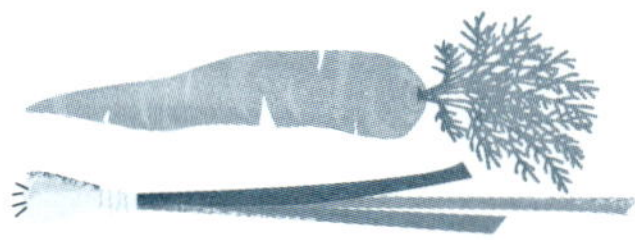

#30–55 Main Dishes

Sausage Spinach Wreath » 44
Dutch Oven Pot Roast » 46
Stuffed Pork Tenderloins in Fresh Tomato Sauce » 47
Stuffed Pork Roast » 48
Sloppy Joes » 49
Stuffed Pork Chops in Mushroom Gravy » 50
Best-Ever Bratwurst » 51
Homemade Dutch Oven Pizza » 52
Pork and Stuffing » 53
The King's Chicken » 54
Catalina Chicken » 55
Chicken Pillows » 56
Teriyaki-Barbecue Chicken » 57
Dutch Oven Mutton » 57
Chicken Roll-Ups » 58
Favorite Dutch Oven Lasagna » 59
Stuffed Flank Steak » 60
Sweet-and-Sour Dutch Oven » 61
Shepherd's Pie » 62
Corned Beef Macaroni » 63
Hamburger Rice Casserole » 64

Sausage-Zucchini Rice Casserole » 65
Easy Chicken and Rice » 66
Chile Verde » 67
Meat and Cheese–Stuffed Manicotti » 68
Apricot and Raspberry–Glazed Cornish Hens » 69

#56–61 Side Dishes

Cabbage Rolls » 72
Potatoes, Onion, and Bacon » 73
Honey-Glazed Carrots » 74
Corn on the Cob » 75
Cheesy Potatoes » 76
Dutch Oven Potatoes » 77

#62–72 Sauces, Soups & Stews

Creamy White Mushroom Sauce » 80
Creamy Parmesan Sauce » 81
Fresh Tomato Sauce » 82
White Chili » 83
Tortilla Soup » 84
Good Ol' Dutch Oven Chili » 85
Dutch Oven Stew » 86
Kvetcher Stew » 87
Lamb Stew » 88
Chunky Chicken Soup » 89
Hamburger Soup » 90

#73–101 Desserts

Raspberry-Peach Pie » 92
Cherry Pie » 94
Pear-Raspberry Pie » 96
Pecan Pie » 97
Lemonheads Pie » 98
Dump Cobbler » 99
Chocolate Cake » 100
Southern-Style Peach Cobbler » 101
Raspberry-Peach Cobbler » 102
Banana Cake » 103
Chocolate-Peppermint Cake » 104
Devil's Food Cake » 105
Apple Spice Cake » 106
Lemon-Orange Cake » 107
Carrot Cake » 108
Zucchini-Carrot Cake » 109
Pumpkin Spice Cake » 110
Oatmeal Cobbler » 111
Pumpkin Crumble » 112
Apple Crunch » 113
Apple Cinnamon Cake » 114
Caramel Apple Cobbler » 115
White Chocolate Cheesecake » 116
Peachy Dump Cake » 117
Strawberry Torte » 118
Smacos » 120
Snack Cake » 121
S'mores Brownies » 122
Sweet Poached Pears » 123

Notes » 124
About the Author » 128

Helpful Hints

- When purchasing a Dutch oven, look for lumps in the casting. Lumps cause hot spots you want to avoid. Look at the thickness of all sides of a Dutch oven. If one side is thinner than the other, it will not cook evenly and your results will be poor. Also, make sure the lid sits flat and does not rock to ensure there is a good seal when cooking. However, if the lid moves side to side slightly, that is fine.
- The Camp Chef Ultimate Dutch Oven, no longer produced by this company, is a special Dutch oven designed for convection cooking, and was made in either aluminum or cast iron. It has a center cone and two racks, one on the bottom for cooking meat and one near the top for cooking vegetables. This oven has many other uses, such as cooking pies and cakes. I use the Camp Chef Ultimate for the Chocolate Cake (page 100) because it is such a moist cake that it does not get done in the middle and burns on the edges when cooked in a regular Dutch oven. It comes out more like a Bundt cake.
- All Dutch ovens come coated with wax to protect them during shipping (unless they have been preseasoned). To season a new Dutch oven, scrub off all the wax and then coat with shortening. Place the Dutch oven, upside down, in a barbecue or an oven (to allow shortening to drip off when heating) and heat to 400 degrees for 30 minutes. This begins to make the nonstick surface for which Dutch ovens are famous. Let the oven cool naturally, and when you can touch it with your hands, place the lid back on the Dutch oven and let it continue to cool. The more you use

the oven, the more seasoned or nonstick it will become. Depending on the frequency of use, you may have to season several times a year. If the oven starts to smell rancid, do the whole seasoning process again.

- When you clean a Dutch oven after it has been seasoned, don't use soap. The soap pulls the seasoning out and you will have to season it again. Use really hot water and a plastic scrubbing pad. Never use anything metal. Metal will scrape away the oven's nonstick surface.

- Store a Dutch oven with something between the lid and the pot, such as a rolled-up paper towel. This allows air to flow through it during storage and helps keep the oven from becoming rancid. If the oven gives off a funny pungent smell, you know it is rancid and needs to be seasoned again. If you use your oven year-round, it will not become rancid. If your oven becomes rusty, you are not using it often enough. Scrub the rust off with an SOS pad, dry, and then season it again.

- Use your Dutch oven year-round; just set it up anywhere it will be protected from wind, such as a patio, garage, or even your home oven. Wind carries the heat away, so it is important to be in a wind-free area.

- Charcoal briquettes, or coals, are used in all of the recipes in this book, and heat control is important for Dutch oven use. Take the size of the oven, such as a 12-inch pot, then double that number to 24. This gives you the number of coals to start with to reach 350 degrees of heat. A 14-inch oven would be 28, a 16-inch would be 32, and so on. Place 10 coals under the Dutch oven and put the rest on top of the lid. Each additional coal placed on the oven adds approximately 20–25 degrees. For baking, put most of the heat on the lid. For frying, put most of the heat on the bottom. You will almost never put a coal in the center of the oven (bottom or lid) as it will make a hot spot and burn food, causing poor results.

- Be mindful of the size of your coals so your heat doesn't drop. When coals are the size of a quarter, it's time to replace them with new ones.
- Rotate the Dutch oven every 10 minutes by moving the lid counterclockwise and bottom clockwise. This will help to cook more evenly, especially with cakes and breads.
- When reducing sauces or liquids in a recipe, place moisture managers between the lid and the Dutch oven or use clothespins to help hold the lid ajar. This allows the moisture to escape.
- You may use a Dutch oven in your indoor oven. To use a cast iron oven that has legs, just pull the indoor oven rack out far enough that you can turn the legs on your camp oven to fit between the wires on the rack. Then push it back in the indoor oven and begin the cooking process. If you have a Dutch oven that is meant to be used in an indoor oven, there will be no legs. Just place it in the oven and cook at the temperature in the recipe, no coals needed. There are also Dutch ovens that are covered with porcelain that are specifically made for use in your indoor oven. The cooking times should be about the same whether cooking with coals or in your home oven.
- Experiment with your Dutch oven and get creative with your recipes. You may even want to enter a Dutch oven cook-off. Look at the International Dutch Oven Society website, www.idos.org, for a cook-off near you.

#1–11

BREAKFAST

#1

Cinnamon Rolls

14-INCH DUTCH OVEN • 350 DEGREES • MAKES 10–12 ROLLS

½ cup	**sugar**
¾ cup	**warm water**
2 tablespoons	**active dry yeast**
1 cup	**milk**
½ cup	**potato flakes**
¾ cup	**butter, softened, divided**
1 teaspoon	**salt**
2	**eggs**
4 to 4½ cups	**flour, divided**
3 teaspoons	**cinnamon**
1½ cups	**brown sugar**
1½ cups	**raisins, optional**
¾ cup	**chopped pecans, optional**
1 container (16 ounces)	**vanilla or cream cheese frosting**

In a large mixing bowl, combine sugar, water, yeast, and milk; let sit for 5 minutes. Add potato flakes and mix well. Mix in ½ cup butter, salt, eggs, and 2 cups flour; beat until well combined. Add remaining flour to form a soft, elastic dough. Place dough in a lightly oiled bowl, turning to coat. Cover with a cloth and let rise in a warm area until double in size. Punch down dough and roll out on a lightly floured surface into a 9 x 11-inch rectangle, about ¼ inch thick. Spread with remaining butter and sprinkle with cinnamon, brown sugar, raisins, and pecans, if using.

Beginning with the long side, roll up dough and pinch the edge together to seal. Cut into 10 to 12 even slices using thread or kitchen string. Place dough slices in Dutch oven prepared with nonstick cooking spray. Cover with a clean cloth and let rise in a warm, draft-free area until double in size. Cover with the lid and bake for 25–30 minutes, or until golden brown, using 12 coals underneath the oven and 16 on top. Frost rolls while still warm.

#2

Sticky Buns

12-INCH DUTCH OVEN • 350 DEGREES • MAKES 16 BUNS

1 cup	**hot milk**
1 tablespoon	**butter**
¼ cup	**warm water**
1 tablespoon	**sugar**
1 tablespoon	**active dry yeast**
3½ cups	**flour, divided**
¼ teaspoon	**salt**
1	**egg, beaten**
½ cup	**butter, melted**
1 cup	**brown sugar**
1 bag (10 ounces)	**chopped pecans**

In a small bowl, stir together hot milk and butter until butter melts. In a separate bowl, combine water, sugar, and yeast; set aside. In a large mixing bowl, combine half the flour, salt, egg, and milk mixture. Beat for 5 minutes. Mix in yeast mixture and then the remaining flour until well combined. Knead dough on a lightly floured surface for 10 minutes or until dough is elastic. Place in Dutch oven prepared with nonstick cooking spray. Cover with the lid and set in a warm area until double in size.

Remove dough from Dutch oven and roll into a long log, 2 to 3 inches in diameter, on a lightly floured surface. Cut the dough into 16 even-size pieces and roll into balls. Dip balls halfway into melted butter. Coat buttered side of dough balls in brown sugar and then roll in pecans. Sprinkle any remaining sugar and pecans in the bottom of Dutch oven. Place dough balls, sugar-side down, in Dutch oven. Cover with the lid and bake for 35–40 minutes, or until golden brown, using 10 coals underneath the oven and 14 on top. When done, invert sticky buns onto a serving plate. Scrape out any remaining sauce from Dutch oven and drizzle over top of buns.

#3

Apple Dumpling Rolls

12-INCH, 5-INCH DUTCH OVENS • 350 DEGREES • MAKES 12 ROLLS

2 cups	**flour**
1 teaspoon	**salt**
2 teaspoons	**baking powder**
3/4 cup	**shortening**
1/2 cup	**milk**
3 to 4	**Granny Smith apples, peeled and shredded**
	cinnamon, for sprinkling

Sauce:

2 cups	**water**
1 cup	**sugar**
1 cup	**brown sugar**
1/4 cup	**butter**
1/4 teaspoon	**cinnamon**

In a large mixing bowl, combine the flour, salt, and baking powder; cut in shortening until mixture is the size of peas. Add milk and mix until a soft dough forms. On a lightly floured surface, roll dough out into a 12 x 16-inch rectangle, about 1/4 inch thick. Scatter apples evenly over top and sprinkle with cinnamon. Beginning with the longer side, roll up the dough like a jelly roll and cut into 12 even slices using thread or kitchen string. Place in 12-inch Dutch oven prepared with nonstick cooking spray.

To make the sauce, add the water, sugars, butter, and cinnamon to 5-inch Dutch oven and heat until melted together and smooth, using 3 coals underneath the oven and 3 around the outside.

Pour the warm sauce around the rolls. Cover with the lid and bake for 30 minutes, using 8 to 10 coals underneath the oven and 16 on top. Serve warm.

#4

Orange Cranberry Rolls

12-INCH DUTCH OVEN • 350 DEGREES • MAKES 16 ROLLS

4 teaspoons	**active dry yeast**
2 cups	**warm water, divided**
7 tablespoons	**sugar, divided**
6 cups	**flour**
4 tablespoons	**instant nonfat dry milk**
2 teaspoons	**salt**
6 tablespoons	**butter, softened**
1 cup	**dried or thawed frozen cranberries**
2 teaspoons	**orange extract**
2	**oranges, zested**

In a small bowl, combine yeast, 1 cup water, and 4 tablespoons sugar; set aside. In a large mixing bowl, combine remaining sugar, flour, dry milk, salt, butter, and cranberries. Stir in the yeast mixture, orange extract, and zest. Add remaining water and knead dough until elastic and cranberries are evenly distributed throughout the dough. Place in a lightly oiled bowl and turn to coat. Cover with a clean cloth and let rise in a warm, draft-free area for 30 minutes, or until double in size.

Punch down dough, cut into 16 even-size pieces, and roll into balls. Place in a warmed* Dutch oven prepared with nonstick cooking spray. Cover with a clean cloth and let rise in a warm, draft-free area until double in size. Cover with the lid and bake for 20–30 minutes or until golden brown, using 10 coals underneath the oven and 14 on top.

*To warm the Dutch oven, place it in the sun or use 4 coals underneath the oven for a few minutes. You want it warm, not hot.

#5

Raisin Bread

10-INCH DUTCH OVEN • 350 DEGREES • MAKES 12 SERVINGS

1½ cups plus 1 tablespoon	**warm water**
4 tablespoons	**sugar**
1 tablespoon	**active dry yeast**
3¾ cups	**flour**
3 tablespoons	**instant nonfat dry milk**
2¼ teaspoons	**salt**
1 tablespoon	**cinnamon**
3 tablespoons	**butter, softened**
1½ cups	**raisins**
½ cup	**chopped nuts of choice, optional**

In a small mixing bowl, combine the water, sugar, and yeast; set aside.

In a large mixing bowl, mix together the flour, dry milk, salt, cinnamon, butter, raisins, and nuts, if using. Add yeast mixture and knead until a soft dough forms. Place in a lightly oiled bowl and turn to coat. Cover with a clean cloth and let rise in a warm, draft-free area for about 45 minutes, or until double in size.

Punch down dough, form into a loaf, and place in the warmed* Dutch oven prepared with nonstick cooking spray. Cover with a clean cloth and let rise in a warm, draft-free area until double in size. Cover with lid and bake for 40 minutes, or until golden brown, using 8 coals underneath the oven and 12 on top.

*To warm the Dutch oven, place it in the sun or use 4 coals underneath the oven for a few minutes. You want it warm, not hot.

#6

Breakfast Rolls

12-INCH DUTCH OVEN • 375 DEGREES • MAKES 16 ROLLS

	oil, for cooking, plus more as needed
1 heaping cup	**cooked, crumbled bacon pieces**
3/4 cup	**chopped fresh mushrooms**
3 tablespoons	**chopped red onion**
9 ounces	**evaporated milk**
6 tablespoons	**butter**
1/2 cup	**water**
4 1/2 cups	**flour**
5 1/4 tablespoons	**sugar**
1 1/2 teaspoons	**salt**
3 teaspoons	**active dry yeast**
3/4 cup	**shredded medium cheddar cheese**

Drizzle a small amount of oil in the bottom of Dutch oven. Add the bacon, mushrooms, and onion and cook until mushrooms are tender, using 9 coals underneath the oven. Remove the mixture from Dutch oven and set aside, leaving any remaining oil.

Add the milk and butter to Dutch oven and heat until butter is melted. Pour into a large mixing bowl and add water. Add the flour, sugar, salt, yeast, cheese, and bacon mixture; mix well, kneading 2–5 minutes. Place dough in a large lightly oiled bowl and turn to coat. Cover with a clean cloth and set in a warm, draft-free area; let rise until double in size.

Punch down dough, divide into 16 even-size pieces, and roll into balls. Place in same Dutch oven prepared with nonstick cooking spray. Cover with lid and let rise until double in size. When rolls have risen, bake for 30–40 minutes, until golden brown, using 9 coals underneath the oven and 15 on top; replace coals as needed.

#7

Cinnamon Pull-Aparts

12-INCH DUTCH OVEN • 350 DEGREES • MAKES 16 SERVINGS

2 cups	**warm water**
1/3 cup	**sugar**
2 tablespoons	**active dry yeast**
1/3 cup	**oil, plus more as needed**
1 1/2 teaspoons	**salt**
1	**egg**
2/3 cup	**instant nonfat dry milk**
5 to 6 cups	**flour, divided**
1/2 cup	**butter, melted**
1 tablespoon	**cinnamon, or to taste**
1 1/2 cups	**brown sugar**

In a large mixing bowl, combine water, sugar, and yeast; set aside for 5 minutes. Add the oil, salt, and egg. In a separate bowl, combine the dry milk with 2 cups flour and add to yeast mixture. Beat until smooth. Add remaining flour, 1 cup at a time, and mix until smooth. Knead dough on a lightly floured surface until elastic, and then place in a lightly oiled bowl and turn to coat. Cover with a clean cloth and let rise until triple in size. Punch down dough, divide into 16 even-size pieces, and roll into balls; dip in melted butter.

In a small bowl, combine cinnamon and brown sugar. Roll balls in cinnamon mixture and then place in a warmed Dutch oven (see tip on page 16) prepared with nonstick cooking spray. Pour any leftover cinnamon mixture over top. Cover with the lid and bake for 15–20 minutes, or until golden, using 10 coals underneath the oven and 14 on top. When done, loosen edges with knife and remove to wire rack to cool.

#8

Breakfast Pizza

14-INCH DUTCH OVEN • 325 DEGREES • MAKES 8 SERVINGS

1 pound	**ground sausage of choice**
1	**green bell pepper, chopped**
1	**medium onion, chopped**
1 package (8 ounces)	**sliced fresh mushrooms**
3 cans (8 ounces each)	**Grands refrigerator biscuits or 1 can refrigerator pizza crust**
10	**eggs, well beaten**
1	**medium tomato, chopped**
1 can (4 ounces)	**sliced black olives**
1/2 pound	**shredded Monterey Jack cheese**
1/2 pound	**shredded mozzarella cheese**
	salsa of choice

Cook and crumble the sausage with bell pepper, onion, and mushrooms in Dutch oven, using 10 coals underneath, until sausage is cooked through. Drain excess grease, remove sausage mixture, and set aside.

In the same Dutch oven, arrange the biscuits over the bottom; flatten and pinch together to form a solid crust. Spoon sausage mixture over top. Pour the eggs over the sausage mixture and sprinkle evenly with tomato, olives, and cheeses. Cover with the lid and bake for 30 minutes, or until bottom of crust is completely cooked and cheese is bubbling, using 8 coals underneath the oven and 16 coals on top; replace coals as needed. Serve with salsa on the side.

#9

Royal Braid

12-INCH DUTCH OVEN • 350 DEGREES • MAKES 16 SERVINGS

2 cups	**warm water**
1 cup plus 3 tablespoons	**sugar, divided**
2 tablespoons plus ½ teaspoon	**active dry yeast**
3 teaspoons	**salt**
3 tablespoons	**butter, softened**
1 cup plus 1–2 tablespoons	**milk, divided**
7½ cups	**flour, divided**
½ cup	**butter, melted, divided**
½ cup	**brown sugar**
1 tablespoon	**cinnamon**
1 cup	**powdered sugar**
½ teaspoon	**vanilla extract**
½ cup	**chopped pecans**

In a large mixing bowl, combine water, ⅔ cup sugar, and yeast. When foamy, add salt, softened butter, 1 cup milk, and 5 cups flour. Stir until well mixed then add remaining flour, ½ cup at a time. Knead on a lightly floured surface until a soft dough forms. Place dough in a lightly oiled bowl and turn to coat. Cover with a clean cloth and set in a warm area for about 45 minutes, or until double in size. Punch down dough and roll out into a 10 x 4-inch rectangle. Brush with half the melted butter.

In a small bowl, combine remaining sugar, brown sugar, and cinnamon; sprinkle evenly over top of dough. Fold dough into thirds and then roll out to a 12 x 4-inch rectangle. Divide the dough lengthwise into three equal pieces and braid together. Bring ends together and pinch to form a circle. Place in Dutch oven prepared with nonstick cooking spray. Cover with lid and bake for 45–55 minutes, or until golden brown, using 10 coals underneath the oven and 14 on top. Remove bread from oven to a wire rack and brush with remaining butter; let cool.

In a small bowl, mix together powdered sugar, remaining 1 to 2 tablespoons milk, and vanilla to desired consistency. Drizzle over cooled braid and then sprinkle with pecans.

#10

Mountain Man Breakfast

12-INCH DUTCH OVEN • 350 DEGREES • MAKES 20 SERVINGS

1 pound	**bacon, cut into 1-inch pieces**
1 pound	**ground sausage of choice, crumbled**
2 packages (24 ounces each)	**frozen diced hash brown potatoes, thawed**
1 container (8 ounces)	**sour cream**
4	**eggs, beaten**
1 pound	**shredded sharp cheddar cheese**

Brown the bacon and sausage in Dutch oven, using 10 coals underneath, until cooked through and bacon is starting to crisp. Stir in hash browns. Cover with lid and bake for 25–30 minutes, using 10 coals underneath the oven and 14 coals on top; replace coals as needed.

In a medium bowl, combine the sour cream and eggs until thoroughly mixed. During the last 5 minutes of cooking, carefully remove lid from Dutch oven and pour the egg mixture evenly over hash browns. Replace lid and continue to cook for 5 minutes, or until eggs are set and cooked through. Remove lid, sprinkle cheese over top, replace lid, and let sit for a few minutes until cheese melts.

#11

Cheesy Breakfast Casserole

12-INCH DUTCH OVEN • 350 DEGREES • MAKES 8 SERVINGS

1 package (24 ounces)	**frozen shredded hash brown potatoes, thawed**
1/3 cup	**butter, melted**
1 cup	**shredded cheddar cheese**
1 cup	**shredded Swiss cheese**
1 cup	**cooked and cubed ham**
6	**eggs**
1/2 cup	**milk**
1/2 teaspoon	**salt**
	finely chopped chives, optional

Warm Dutch oven over 10 coals, and then cook the potatoes in the butter until they start to brown. Spread the potatoes evenly over the bottom of the oven and sprinkle both cheeses and ham over top.

In a medium bowl, beat the eggs, milk, and salt together until well combined. Pour evenly over the ham, cheese, and potatoes. Cover with lid and bake for 30–35 minutes, or until eggs are set and cheese is bubbling, using 10 coals underneath the oven and 14 coals on top. Sprinkle with chives, if using, and serve.

Remember to check the coals and replace any that have become the size of a quarter with a new hot coal.

#12-29

BREADS & ROLLS

#12

Basic White Bread

12-INCH DUTCH OVEN • 350 DEGREES • MAKES 12 SERVINGS

1 cup	**warm water**
2 tablespoons	**sugar**
2 teaspoons	**active dry yeast**
2 3/4 cups	**flour**
2 tablespoons	**instant nonfat dry milk**
1 3/4 teaspoons	**salt**
2 tablespoons	**butter, softened**

In a small bowl, combine water, sugar, and yeast; set aside.

In a large mixing bowl, mix flour, dry milk, and salt. Add butter and the yeast mixture. Knead until a soft dough forms. Place in a lightly oiled bowl and turn to coat. Cover with a clean cloth and let rise in a warm, draft-free area until double in size. Punch down dough and form a loaf. Place in a warmed* Dutch oven prepared with nonstick cooking spray. Cover and let rise until double in size.

Cover with the lid and bake at 350 degrees for 40 minutes, or until golden brown, using 10 coals underneath and 14 on top.

*To warm the Dutch oven, place it in the sun or use 4 coals underneath the oven for a few minutes. You want it warm, not hot.

#13

Potato Bread

10-INCH DUTCH OVEN • 350 DEGREES • MAKES 12 SERVINGS

1 cup plus 2 tablespoons	**warm water**
1½ tablespoons	**sugar**
2 teaspoons	**active dry yeast**
3 cups	**flour**
½ cup	**instant potato flakes**
1½ tablespoons	**nonfat instant dry milk**
1½ teaspoons	**salt**
1½ tablespoons	**butter, softened**

In a small bowl, combine water, sugar, and yeast; set aside.

In a large mixing bowl, mix flour, potato flakes, dry milk, salt, and butter. Add yeast mixture and knead until a soft dough forms. Place in a lightly oiled bowl and turn to coat. Cover with a clean cloth and let rise in a warm, draft-free area until double in size. Punch down dough and form a loaf. Place in a warmed Dutch oven prepared with nonstick cooking spray. Cover and let rise until double in size.

Cover with the lid and bake 40 minutes, or until golden brown, at 350 degrees using 8 coals underneath and 12 on top.

To tell if bread is cooked through, thump the bottom of the loaf and listen for a hollow sound.

#14

Garlic Bread

10-INCH DUTCH OVEN • 350 DEGREES • MAKES 12 SERVINGS

1 cup plus 2 tablespoons	**warm water**
1 tablespoon	**sugar**
2 teaspoons	**active dry yeast**
3 cups	**flour**
1 tablespoon	**instant nonfat dry milk**
1½ teaspoons	**salt**
1 tablespoon	**dried parsley**
1½ to 3 teaspoons	**garlic powder, or to taste**
1 tablespoon	**butter, softened**

In a small bowl, combine water, sugar, and yeast; set aside.

In a large mixing bowl, mix together the flour, dry milk, salt, parsley, and garlic powder. Mix in butter and the yeast mixture and knead until a soft dough forms. Place in a lightly oiled bowl and turn to coat. Cover with a clean cloth and let rise in a warm, draft-free area until double in size. Punch down dough, form into a round loaf, and then place in a warmed Dutch oven prepared with nonstick cooking spray. Cover and let rise until double in size.

Cover with the lid and bake for 40 minutes, or until golden brown, using 8 coals underneath the oven and 12 on top.

Variation: For garlic lovers, try replacing the garlic powder with minced or chopped fresh or dried garlic, to taste.

#15

Easy Onion Soup Bread

12-INCH DUTCH OVEN • 350 DEGREES • MAKES 12 SERVINGS

2 cups plus 1 tablespoon	**buttermilk**
3 tablespoons	**butter, softened**
3 tablespoons	**molasses**
1 envelope	**onion soup mix**
3 3⁄4 cups	**flour**
3⁄4 cup	**cornmeal**
3 teaspoons	**active dry yeast**

In a large mixing bowl, combine the buttermilk, butter, and molasses until well mixed. Add the soup mix, flour, and cornmeal. Add the yeast and knead on a lightly floured surface until a soft dough forms. Place in a lightly oiled bowl and turn to coat, or leave on floured surface. Cover with a clean cloth and let rise in a warm, draft-free area until double in size. Punch down dough and form into a round loaf. Place in a warmed* Dutch oven prepared with nonstick cooking spray. Cover and let rise until double in size.

Cover with the lid and bake for 40 minutes, or until golden brown, using 10 coals underneath and 14 on top.

*To warm the Dutch oven, place it in the sun or use 4 coals underneath the oven for a few minutes. You want it warm, not hot.

You can make your own buttermilk by combining 1 3⁄4 cups milk with 1⁄4 cup lemon juice.

#16

Italian Herb and Cheese Loaf

10-INCH DUTCH OVEN • 350 DEGREES • MAKES 12 SERVINGS

1 cup plus 1 tablespoon	**warm water**
1 tablespoon	**sugar**
1½ teaspoons	**active dry yeast**
2¾ cups	**flour**
1 tablespoon	**instant nonfat dry milk**
1½ teaspoons	**salt**
¼ cup	**freshly grated Parmesan or Asiago cheese**
2 teaspoons	**Italian seasoning**
2 tablespoons	**butter, softened**

In a small bowl, combine water, sugar, and yeast; set aside.

In a large mixing bowl, mix together the flour, dry milk, salt, cheese, and Italian seasoning. Mix in butter and the yeast mixture, and knead until a soft dough forms. Place in a lightly oiled bowl and turn to coat. Cover with a clean cloth and let rise in a warm, draft-free area until double in size. Punch down dough, form into a round loaf, and place in a warmed* Dutch oven prepared with nonstick cooking spray. Cover and let rise until double in size.

Cover with the lid and bake for 40 minutes, or until golden brown, using 8 coals underneath the oven and 12 on top.

*To warm the Dutch oven, place it in the sun or use 4 coals underneath the oven for a few minutes. You want it warm, not hot.

#17

Russian Black Bread

12-INCH DUTCH OVEN • 350 DEGREES • MAKES 16 SERVINGS

2½ cups	**flour**
1 cup	**rye flour**
1 teaspoon	**salt**
2 tablespoons	**brown sugar**
3 tablespoons	**unsweetened cocoa powder**
1 tablespoon	**caraway seeds**
¼ teaspoon	**fennel seeds**
2 teaspoons	**active dry yeast**
4 teaspoons	**Postum, or 1 teaspoon instant coffee granules**
2 tablespoons	**vinegar**
2 tablespoons	**butter, softened**
2 tablespoons	**dark corn syrup**
1½ cups	**hot water**

In a large mixing bowl, combine flour, rye flour, salt, brown sugar, cocoa powder, caraway seeds, fennel seeds, yeast, and Postum. Add the vinegar, butter, corn syrup, and hot water, and knead on a lightly floured surface until a soft dough forms. Place in a lightly oiled bowl and turn to coat. Cover with a clean cloth and let rise in a warm, draft-free area for 30 minutes, or until double in size. Punch down dough and knead on a lightly floured surface until it becomes smooth and holds its shape, about 10 minutes. Note: the longer you knead the dough, the tougher your bread will be. Form into a round loaf and place in Dutch oven prepared with nonstick cooking spray. Cover and let rise in a warm, draft-free area until double in size.

Cover with the lid and bake for 30–40 minutes, or until the crust is a nice dark brown, using 10 coals underneath the oven and 14 on top.

#18

Jalapeño Cheese Bread

12-INCH DUTCH OVEN • 350 DEGREES • MAKES 16 SERVINGS

3 tablespoons	**butter, softened, divided**
3	**eggs, separated into yolks and whites**
3 tablespoons	**sugar**
2 cups	**milk**
⅔ cup	**cornmeal**
⅔ cup	**flour**
1 teaspoon	**salt plus 1 pinch salt, divided**
2 teaspoons	**baking powder**
1	**jalapeño, thinly sliced, optional**
⅓ cup	**shredded jalapeño pepper Jack cheese, plus extra for sprinkling over top**

Preheat Dutch oven using 10 coals underneath the oven. Place 1 tablespoon butter in oven to melt.

In a large mixing bowl, combine remaining butter, egg yolks, and sugar; mix well. Add milk, cornmeal, flour, 1 teaspoon salt, and baking powder. Mix until well combined. Carefully fold in the jalapeño, if using.

In a separate bowl, whip together the egg whites and the pinch of salt until soft peaks form. Fold gently into cornmeal mixture along with the cheese until combined.

Transfer mixture to preheated Dutch oven, cover with the lid, and bake for 20–25 minutes, using 10 coals underneath the oven and 14 on top. Replace coals as needed. Sprinkle more cheese over top during last 5 minutes of baking and let melt.

#19

One-Bowl Dinner Rolls

12-INCH DUTCH OVEN • 375 DEGREES • MAKES 16 ROLLS

2 3/4 to 3 1/4 cups	**flour, divided**
3/4 cup	**sugar**
1/2 teaspoon	**salt**
2 tablespoons	**active dry yeast**
5 1/3 tablespoons	**butter, softened**
2/3 cup	**hot water**
1	**egg, at room temperature, beaten**
1 teaspoon	**garlic powder**
1 teaspoon	**onion powder**
2 teaspoons	**dried rosemary**

In a large mixing bowl, mix together 3/4 cup flour, sugar, salt, and yeast. Add butter and water. Stir until well combined and a thick batter forms. Stir in egg, 1/2 cup flour, garlic powder, onion powder, and rosemary. Knead in bowl, gradually adding enough of the remaining flour until a soft dough forms. Knead for 2 minutes, or until smooth. Cover with a clean cloth and let rise in a warm, draft-free area until double in size. Punch down dough, divide into 16 even-size pieces, and roll into balls. Place dough balls in a warmed* Dutch oven prepared with nonstick cooking spray. Cover and let rise until double in size.

Cover with the lid and bake for 10–15 minutes, or until golden brown, using 10 coals underneath the oven and 16 on top.

*To warm the Dutch oven, place it in the sun or use 4 coals underneath the oven for a few minutes. You want it warm, not hot.

#20

Golden Honey Sourdough Rolls

12-INCH DUTCH OVEN • 350 DEGREES • MAKES 16 ROLLS

2 cups	**scalded milk**
2 tablespoons	**butter**
¼ cup	**honey**
1 tablespoon	**active dry yeast**
4 cups	**Sourdough Starter (page 40)**
2 cups	**wheat flour**
¼ cup	**wheat germ, optional**
2 teaspoons	**baking soda**
2 tablespoons	**salt**
2 tablespoons	**sugar**
2 cups	**all-purpose flour**

In a small mixing bowl, combine milk, butter, and honey; stir until well mixed. Set aside to cool until lukewarm. Add yeast and stir until dissolved. In a large mixing bowl, combine Sourdough Starter, wheat flour, and wheat germ, if using.

In a small bowl, combine baking soda, salt, and sugar; add to sourdough mixture and gently combine. Add yeast mixture and mix well. Cover with a clean cloth and let sit 30 minutes. Stir down dough and gradually add remaining all-purpose flour until too stiff to stir with a spoon (amount of flour may vary). Place on a lightly floured surface and knead until smooth and elastic then place in a lightly oiled bowl and turn to coat. Cover and let rise in a warm, draft-free area until double in size. Punch down dough, divide into 16 even-size pieces, and roll into balls. Place in a warmed* Dutch oven prepared with nonstick cooking spray, cover, and let rise until double in size.

Cover with the lid and bake for 20 minutes, or until golden brown, using 10 coals underneath the oven and 14 on top. Remove from Dutch oven and cool on a wire rack.

#21

Simple French Bread

12-INCH DUTCH OVEN • 350 DEGREES • MAKES 12 SERVINGS

3 cups	**warm water**
2 tablespoons	**sugar**
2 tablespoons	**active dry yeast**
1 tablespoon	**salt**
8 cups	**flour, divided**

In a large bowl, combine water, sugar, yeast, and salt and set aside 5 minutes. Add 4 cups flour and mix well. Gradually add remaining flour and mix until a soft dough forms and then knead until elastic. Cover with a clean cloth and let rise 10 minutes, then knead 5 minutes. (The longer you knead, the tougher the crust will be, thus creating a true French bread.) Form a loaf and place in a warmed* Dutch oven prepared with nonstick cooking spray. Cover and let rise until double in size.

Cover with the lid and bake 30 minutes at 350 degrees using 10 coals underneath and 14 on top.

*To warm the Dutch oven, place it in the sun or use 4 coals underneath the oven for a few minutes. You want it warm, not hot.

#22

Basic Dinner Rolls

12-INCH DUTCH OVEN • 350 DEGREES • MAKES 16 ROLLS

2½ cups	**warm water**
5 tablespoons	**sugar**
2 tablespoons	**active dry yeast**
1 tablespoon	**salt**
5 tablespoons	**oil**
7 to 7 ½ cups	**flour, divided**

In a large mixing bowl, combine water, sugar, and yeast and set aside 5 minutes. Add salt and oil and mix well. Add 4 cups flour and mix until smooth. Gradually add enough remaining flour, about 3 to 3½ cups, until a soft dough forms. Knead until elastic. Place in a lightly oiled bowl and turn to coat. Cover with a clean cloth and let rise in a warm, draft-free area until double in size. Punch down dough and knead again. Form 16 balls and place in a warmed* Dutch oven prepared with nonstick cooking spray. Cover and let rise until double in size.

Cover with the lid and bake 30 minutes at 350 degrees using 10 coals underneath and 14 on top. Immediately remove from Dutch oven to cool.

*To warm the Dutch oven, place it in the sun or use 4 coals underneath the oven for a few minutes. You want it warm, not hot.

#23

Rolls Supreme

12-INCH DUTCH OVEN • 425 DEGREES • MAKES 16 ROLLS

1¼ cups	**warm water, divided**
¼ cup	**sugar**
1 tablespoon	**active dry yeast**
½ teaspoon	**salt**
1 tablespoon	**Salad Supreme seasoning**
½ cup	**butter, melted**
2	**eggs**
3 to 5 cups	**flour**
1	**egg white, slightly whipped**

In a small bowl, combine ¼ cup water, sugar, and yeast and set aside.

In a large mixing bowl, mix remaining water, salt, Salad Supreme, butter, and 2 eggs. Stir in 1 cup flour until well blended. Add yeast mixture. Gradually add remaining flour and knead until smooth. Cover with a clean cloth and let rise in a warm, draft-free area 45 minutes, or until double in size. Punch down dough and form 16 balls. Place in Dutch oven prepared with nonstick cooking spray. Cover and let rise until double in size. Brush with egg white, then sprinkle with more Salad Supreme, if desired.

Cover with the lid and bake 25 minutes, or until golden brown, at 425 degrees using 10 coals underneath and 19 on top.

#24

Parmesan Herb Twists

12-INCH DUTCH OVEN • 375 DEGREES • MAKES 16 ROLLS

1 cup	**warm milk**
1 cup	**warm water**
4 1/2 teaspoons	**active dry yeast**
6 tablespoons	**butter, melted**
3	**eggs, well beaten**
1 teaspoon	**salt**
1/2 cup	**sugar**
1 teaspoon	**garlic powder**
1 teaspoon	**onion powder**
1 teaspoon	**crushed dried rosemary**
3 tablespoons	**freshly grated Parmesan cheese, plus extra for topping**
6 1/2 cups	**flour, divided**

In a large mixing bowl, stir together the milk, water, and yeast. Add butter, eggs, salt, sugar, garlic powder, onion powder, rosemary, and Parmesan cheese. Add 3 cups flour and mix well to combine. Gradually add remaining flour and knead until a soft dough forms. Place in a lightly oiled bowl and turn to coat. Cover with a towel and let rise in a warm, draft-free area until double in size.

Punch down dough, divide into 16 even-size pieces, and roll into balls. Divide each ball in half and roll halves into 6-inch ropes. Twist two ropes together, pinching the ends to seal, and place in Dutch oven prepared with nonstick cooking spray. Repeat with remaining ropes. Cover and let rise until double in size.

Cover with the lid and bake for 20–30 minutes, or until golden brown, using 12 coals underneath the oven and 22 on top. Remove from Dutch oven and sprinkle with more cheese. Cool on a wire rack.

#25

Pumpernickel Rolls

10-INCH DUTCH OVEN • 350 DEGREES • MAKES 12 ROLLS

1¼ cups	**warm water**
1 tablespoon	**sugar**
4½ teaspoons	**active dry yeast**
1 cup	**rye flour**
1 cup	**wheat flour**
¼ cup	**molasses**
2 tablespoons	**cocoa powder**
1 tablespoon	**caraway seeds**
1¼ teaspoons	**salt**
1½ cups plus 2 tablespoons	**flour, divided**

In a large mixing bowl, combine water, sugar, and yeast; set aside for 5 minutes. Add rye and wheat flours, molasses, cocoa powder, caraway seeds, and salt; mix well. Stir in 1 cup flour then place on a lightly floured surface. Knead for 5 minutes, gradually adding more flour only if necessary, until dough is smooth and elastic. Place in a lightly oiled bowl and turn to coat. Cover with a clean cloth and let rise in a warm, draft-free area for 60 minutes, or until double in size. Punch down dough, divide into 12 even-size pieces, and roll into balls. Place dough balls in a warmed* Dutch oven prepared with nonstick cooking spray. Cover and let rise 30 minutes, or until double in size.

Cover with the lid and bake for 30 minutes, or until tops are golden brown, using 8 coals underneath the oven and 12 on top.

*To warm the Dutch oven, place it in the sun or use 4 coals underneath the oven for a few minutes. You want it warm, not hot.

#26

Licorice Dill Rolls

14-INCH DUTCH OVEN • 350 DEGREES • MAKES 16 ROLLS

7 tablespoons	**sugar, divided**
4 teaspoons	**active dry yeast**
2 cups	**hot water, divided**
6 cups	**flour**
4 tablespoons	**instant nonfat dry milk**
2 teaspoons	**salt**
4 teaspoons	**dill weed**
2 teaspoons	**fennel seeds**
6 tablespoons	**butter, melted**

In a small bowl, mix 3 tablespoons sugar, yeast, and 1 cup hot water and set aside.

In a large mixing bowl, combine flour, milk, salt, dill, and fennel. Add yeast mixture, butter, and remaining water. Mix until dough is elastic. Place dough in a lightly oiled bowl and turn to coat. Cover with a clean cloth and let rise in a warm, draft-free area 30 minutes, or until double in size. Punch down dough and form into 16 balls. Place in a warmed* Dutch oven prepared with nonstick cooking spray. Cover and let rise until double in size.

Cover with the lid and bake at 350 degrees using 10–12 coals underneath and 16–18 on top. Bake 20–25 minutes, or until done.

*To warm the Dutch oven, place it in the sun or use 4 coals underneath the oven for a few minutes. You want it warm, not hot.

#27

Crescent Rolls

12-INCH DUTCH OVEN • 350 DEGREES • MAKES 16 ROLLS

1⅓ cups	**scalded milk**
2 tablespoons	**butter**
4 tablespoons	**sugar**
1 teaspoon	**salt**
4½ teaspoons	**yeast**
¼ cup	**warm water**
2	**eggs, well beaten**
4½ cups	**flour**

In a small bowl, combine milk, butter, sugar, and salt. Let cool to room temperature.

In a large mixing bowl, combine yeast and water, and then add cooled milk mixture and eggs. Add 2½ cups flour and mix until well blended. Gradually add remaining flour until a soft dough forms. Place in a lightly oiled bowl and turn to coat. Cover with a clean cloth and let rise in a warm, draft-free area until double in size. Punch down dough and divide into two equal parts. Roll each out to a 12-inch circle on a floured surface. Cut each circle into eight triangles and roll up, starting with the wide end and finishing with the point, then bend ends in slightly to form a crescent shape. Place in Dutch oven prepared with nonstick cooking spray.

Cover with the lid and bake 20–25 minutes, or until golden brown, at 350 degrees using 10 coals underneath and 14 on top.

#28

Sourdough Starter

MAKES 3 CUPS

2 cups flour
2 cups warm water
1 envelope active dry yeast

Combine flour, warm water, and yeast in a large glass bowl or jar (not metal) and mix together until well blended. Cover loosely with a clean cloth or lid (do not tighten or jar may explode) and leave in a warm place (80–85 degrees) for 48 hours to ferment.

When ready to use, give starter a good stir. Remove amount required by the recipe and replenish starter with equal amounts of flour and water. For example, if 2 cups of starter were removed, replace with 1 cup flour and 1 cup warm water; mix well. Let stand in a warm place for a few hours until it bubbles. Cover loosely and refrigerate. Use and replenish every few weeks.

When measuring flour, spoon into measuring cup and level off. Do not scoop with the cup.

#29

Sourdough Bread

14-INCH DUTCH OVEN • 375 DEGREES

3 cups	**hot water (between 80 and 100 degrees)**
2 tablespoons	**sugar**
2 tablespoons	**active dry yeast**
1 tablespoon	**salt**
2 cups	**Sourdough Starter (facing page)**
9 cups	**flour, divided**

In a large mixing bowl, combine water, sugar, and yeast; set aside for 5 minutes. Stir in salt and Sourdough Starter. Add 4 cups flour and stir until dough is smooth. Gradually add enough of the remaining flour to make the dough workable and not sticky. Knead on a lightly floured surface until smooth and elastic. Place in a lightly oiled bowl and turn to coat. Cover with a clean cloth and let rise in a warm, draft-free area for 60 minutes, or until double in size. Punch down dough, remove from bowl, and divide and shape dough into 2 oblong loaves. Place in a warmed* Dutch oven prepared with nonstick cooking spray. Cover and let rise until double in size.

Cover with the lid and bake for 30–40 minutes, using 10 coals underneath the oven and 16 on top. You can tell the bread is done if it sounds hollow when you tap the bottom of the loaf.

*To warm the Dutch oven, place it in the sun or use 4 coals underneath the oven for a few minutes. You want it warm, not hot.

#30–55

MAIN DISHES

#30

Sausage Spinach Wreath

12-INCH CAMP CHEF ULTIMATE* DUTCH OVEN • 400 DEGREES • MAKES 12–16 SERVINGS

½ pound	**ground pork, browned and drained**
½ pound	**pork sausage, browned and drained**
1 package (8 ounces)	**cream cheese, softened**
1 can (8 ounces)	**water chestnuts, drained and chopped**
1 packet (1.4 ounces)	**Knorr Vegetable Recipe Mix**
6 ounces	**chopped frozen spinach, thawed**
1 or 2	**green onions, green stalks only, chopped**
2 (10 x 15-inch) sheets	**frozen puff pastry, thawed**

In a large bowl, mix together all of the ingredients except puff pastry; cover and set aside. Cut off corners of both sheets of pastry, making them into 10-inch circles. Cut each circle into eight even wedges, for a total of 16.

Cover Dutch oven rack with parchment paper and arrange seven pastry wedges in a circle with wide edges touching or slightly overlapping and points facing out. Arrange seven more wedges in the center of the circle, matching wide ends with wedges already in place, slightly overlapping, points facing center (points will overlap). Lightly press the side edges together to seal. Discard unused pastry.

Spoon meat mixture evenly over the wide overlapped edges of the pastry to form a circle. Beginning with last pastry wedge that was placed in the center, lift point and lay straight across meat mixture, tucking the point underneath the pastry. Lift the point from opposite outside wedge diagonally across point of previous wedge and lay across meat mixture, tucking point underneath pastry. Continue alternating points until a wreath is formed; some filling will show.

Cut three or four slits in the center of the parchment paper so that it will slide easily over the center convection cone and place rack in a warmed** Dutch oven. Cover with the lid and bake for 40–50 minutes, or until golden brown, using 15 coals underneath the oven and 20 on top.

*Tie a string onto the Ultimate rack to help lift wreath out of the oven when baked.

**To warm the Dutch oven, place it in the sun or use 4 coals underneath the oven for a few minutes. You want it warm, not hot.

#31

Dutch Oven Pot Roast

12-INCH DUTCH OVEN • 350 DEGREES • MAKES 6–8 SERVINGS

1 envelope	**dry onion soup mix**
1 (3- to 4-pound)	**beef roast**
1½ cups	**water, plus extra as needed, divided**
2	**beef bouillon cubes**
½ pound	**baby carrots**
8 to 10	**medium red or new potatoes**
2 tablespoons	**flour**

Preheat Dutch oven using all 24 coals underneath the oven.

Rub dry soup mix over the entire roast, place in preheated oven, and sear until browned on all sides. Add 1 cup water and the bouillon. Cover with the lid and bake for 30 minutes, using 10 coals underneath the oven and 14 on top. Replace coals as needed to maintain cooking temperature.

Check and add water as needed, keeping the bottom of the oven covered with liquid. Add carrots and potatoes, cover, and continue to bake for 30 more minutes, or until vegetables are tender and roast is cooked to an internal temperature of 160 degrees. Remove roast from oven to a serving platter and let rest for a few minutes. Remove vegetables to a serving bowl and cover to keep warm.

To make a gravy, bring drippings in Dutch oven to a boil; add flour and remaining ½ cup water, stirring constantly until smooth and starting to thicken. Spoon gravy over roast and vegetables to serve.

#32

Stuffed Pork Tenderloins in Fresh Tomato Sauce

12-INCH DUTCH OVEN • 350 DEGREES • MAKES 8 SERVINGS

2/3 can (8 ounces)	**whole water chestnuts, drained and chopped**
6 to 8 ounces	**frozen chopped spinach, partially thawed**
1 package (8 ounces)	**cream cheese, softened**
1 or 2	**green onions, green stalks only, chopped**
1 packet (1.4 ounces)	**Knorr Vegetable Recipe Mix**
2 (1-pound)	**pork tenderloins**
	vegetable oil, for browning
1 recipe	**Fresh Tomato Sauce (page 82)**

In a medium mixing bowl, combine water chestnuts, spinach, cream cheese, green onions, and Knorr mix; set aside.

With a sharp knife, make a lengthwise cut down the center of each tenderloin, cutting two-thirds of the way through. Press sides apart and make another lengthwise cut down the middle of each side, cutting only two-thirds of the way through.

Brown the tenderloins on all sides in a small amount of oil in Dutch oven, using 20 to 24 coals underneath the oven. Remove tenderloins and set aside to cool. Once cooled, divide the spinach mixture in half and spread evenly over each tenderloin. Roll up the tenderloins tightly, like a jelly roll, and tie each one with kitchen twine to secure at each end and in the middle. Place in Dutch oven and pour tomato sauce over top. Cover with the lid and bake for 35–40 minutes, or until the internal temperature reaches 160 degrees, using 10 coals underneath the oven and 14 on top. Replace coals as needed. Serve with warm sauce drizzled over top.

#33

Stuffed Pork Roast

14-INCH DUTCH OVEN • 350 DEGREES • MAKES 8 SERVINGS

1 (2- to 3-pound)	**boneless pork roast**
	salt and pepper, to taste
2 tablespoons	**toasted pine nuts**
½ cup	**chopped fresh mint**
½ cup	**chopped fresh parsley**
6 to 8 cloves	**garlic, peeled and crushed**
½ cup	**freshly grated Parmesan cheese**
1	**lemon, juiced**
2 tablespoons	**olive oil, divided**
1 recipe	**Fresh Tomato Sauce (page 82)**

Place meat on a cutting board and slice lengthwise down the center of the roast, cutting only two-thirds of the way through. Press each side apart and make another lengthwise cut down the center of each side, cutting only two-thirds through. Pound roast until it lays flat. Season with salt and pepper.

In a small bowl, combine nuts, mint, parsley, garlic, cheese, lemon juice, and 1 tablespoon oil. Stir together until combined and spread evenly over roast. Roll up the roast tightly, like a jelly roll, and tie together with kitchen twine to secure at each end and in the middle. Season with more salt and pepper.

Heat Dutch oven using 10 coals underneath the oven and 16 on top. Add remaining oil and brown roast on all sides. Add tomato sauce, cover, and bring to a boil. Reduce heat to a simmer by removing several coals from the top.

Simmer gently for 60 minutes, or until internal temperature reaches 145 degrees, turning roast a few times during cooking. Replace coals as needed.

Remove roast from Dutch oven to a serving plate and let rest for 15 minutes. Remove and discard twine and slice roast into ½-inch-thick pieces. Serve with warm sauce drizzled over top.

#34

Sloppy Joes

12-INCH DUTCH OVEN • 350 DEGREES • MAKES 4–6 SERVINGS

1 pound	**ground beef**
1 can (10.75 ounces)	**chicken gumbo soup**
½ cup	**ketchup**
⅛ cup	**mustard**
½	**medium onion, chopped**
1 can (8 ounces)	**tomato sauce**
2 tablespoons	**Worcestershire sauce**
4 to 6	**hamburger buns**

In Dutch oven, brown the ground beef until cooked through, using 30 coals underneath the oven; drain the grease. Add the soup, ketchup, mustard, onion, tomato sauce, and Worcestershire sauce. Mix to combine. Remove enough coals from underneath the oven to achieve a simmer. Cover with the lid and simmer for 30 minutes, stirring occasionally to prevent burning. Serve in buns.

#35

Stuffed Pork Chops in Mushroom Gravy

12-INCH DUTCH OVEN • 350 DEGREES • MAKES 4 SERVINGS

1 package (8 ounces)	**sliced fresh mushrooms, divided**
3 cups	**breadcrumbs**
3 to 4	**green onions, thinly sliced**
1/3	**red bell pepper, diced**
2 cloves	**garlic, minced**
1 stalk	**celery, diced**
1/2 teaspoon	**salt**
1 3/4 teaspoons	**ground sage**
1/2 cup	**shelled and roasted sunflower seeds**
6 tablespoons	**butter, melted**
1/2 cup	**evaporated milk**
4	**center-cut pork loin chops, about 1 inch thick**
1/2 cup	**pork rub, divided**
1 packet	**onion gravy mix**

In a large mixing bowl, add half the mushrooms, the breadcrumbs, green onions, bell pepper, garlic, celery, salt, sage, sunflower seeds, butter, and milk. Mix together until the breadcrumbs are completely moistened and then place in refrigerator or cooler.

Using a sharp knife, cut a horizontal slit about two-thirds of the way through each pork chop to make a pocket for the stuffing. Use 1/4 cup of the pork rub to season and rub on both sides of each chop. Place chops in heated Dutch oven, using 20 coals underneath the oven, and sear on both sides. Remove chops from oven to a plate and refrigerate until ready to stuff.

Make gravy according to package directions; stir in remaining pork rub and mushrooms. Remove pork chops and filling from the refrigerator. Divide the filling evenly between the chops and stuff; secure with toothpicks if necessary. Place chops back in Dutch oven with the gravy. Cover with the lid and bake for 30–40 minutes, or until the internal temperature reaches 165 degrees, using 10 coals underneath the oven and 14 on top. Replace coals as needed. Serve with mushroom gravy.

#36

Best-Ever Bratwurst

12-INCH DUTCH OVEN • 350 DEGREES • MAKES 6 SERVINGS

4 bratwurst, cut into 1-inch slices
1 head cabbage, shredded
3 large carrots, shredded

Prepare Dutch oven with nonstick cooking spray and then cook bratwurst using 14 coals underneath. Add cabbage and carrots. Cover with the lid and add 10 coals on top. Bake 5 minutes, or until vegetables are cooked, but still firm.

#37

Homemade Dutch Oven Pizza

12-INCH DUTCH OVEN • 425 DEGREES • MAKES 8 SERVINGS

3/4 cup	**warm water**
2 tablespoons	**vegetable oil**
2 cups	**flour**
1/2 teaspoon	**sugar**
1/2 teaspoon	**salt**
2 teaspoons	**active dry yeast**
	tomato or pizza sauce of choice
	favorite pizza toppings
2 cups	**shredded mozzarella cheese**

In a large mixing bowl, mix together the water, oil, flour, sugar, salt, and yeast until well combined. Cover with a clean cloth and let rise in a warm, draft-free area for 20–30 minutes, or until double in size.

Place dough in Dutch oven prepared with nonstick cooking spray. Flatten gently, pressing from the center of the oven to the edges and slightly up the sides to form a crust. Spread desired amount of tomato sauce over dough and layer with your favorite toppings and cheese. Cover with the lid and bake for 20–25 minutes, or until cheese is melted and bubbly and crust is cooked on the bottom, using 10 coals underneath the oven and 18 on top. When done, carefully remove pizza from oven by tilting gently while a helper slides spatulas under the crust and guides it onto a rack or large plate.

Need a bigger pizza? Double ingredients and bake in a 14-inch Dutch oven at 425 degrees, using 12 coals underneath the oven and 20 on top.

To make removing the pizza from Dutch oven a lot easier, fit and layer the bottom and sides of the oven with a large round piece of parchment paper before adding the dough. This way you can lift the cooked pizza out of the oven by using the parchment paper as handles.

#38

Pork and Stuffing

12-INCH DUTCH OVEN • 350 DEGREES • MAKES 12 SERVINGS

2½ pound	**pork roast, cut into 1-inch pieces**
2 cans (10.5 ounces each)	**condensed cream of mushroom soup**
1 package (8 ounces)	**sliced mushrooms**
2 boxes (6 ounces each)	**stuffing mix**

Brown roast pieces in Dutch oven using 30 coals underneath only, and then drain. Add soup and stir. Remove enough coals to reach a simmer and bake 30–45 minutes to tenderize roast. Layer mushrooms over top.

In a saucepan, make stuffing according to package directions. Spoon over mushrooms. Cover with the lid and bake 30 minutes at 350 degrees using 10 new coals underneath and 14 new coals on top.

#39

The King's Chicken

12-INCH DUTCH OVEN • 350 DEGREES • MAKES 8–10 SERVINGS

1 tablespoon	**butter**
1/2 cup	**shredded Monterey Jack cheese**
1/4 cup	**chopped fresh chives**
1/4 cup	**chopped fresh parsley**
1 1/2 teaspoons	**salt**
1 teaspoon	**orange zest, divided**
1/8 teaspoon	**pepper**
1/4 cup	**chopped fresh spinach**
2	**eggs**
1/2 cup	**orange juice**
4 tablespoons	**flour**
1 cup	**breadcrumbs**
6	**boneless, skinless chicken breasts, flattened to 1/4 inch thick**
1 recipe	**Creamy White Mushroom Sauce (page 80)**

In a medium mixing bowl, combine butter, cheese, chives, parsley, salt, 1/2 teaspoon orange zest, pepper, and spinach; form into six finger-size pieces and chill until firm.

In a separate bowl, mix together the eggs, orange juice, and flour until well combined. Pour batter into Dutch oven and heat, using 10 coals underneath the oven, stirring constantly until slightly thickened. Remove from heat and set aside to cool. When Dutch oven is cool enough to handle, pour batter into a separate bowl and wipe Dutch oven out with a clean lint-free cloth.

In a small bowl, thoroughly mix breadcrumbs and remaining orange zest together; set aside.

Roll 1 of the chilled filling pieces in each flattened chicken breast and secure with a toothpick, if necessary. Dip in batter and roll in breadcrumb mixture to coat. Place in Dutch oven prepared with nonstick cooking spray. Cover with the lid and bake for 45 minutes, using 10 coals underneath the oven and 14 on top. Serve with Creamy White Mushroom Sauce over top.

#40

Catalina Chicken

12-INCH DUTCH OVEN • 350 DEGREES • MAKES 8–10 SERVINGS

3 to 4 pounds	**chicken leg and thigh pieces, skin removed***
1 bottle (24 ounces)	**Catalina salad dressing**

Layer chicken in Dutch oven and pour dressing evenly over top. Cover with the lid and bake for 60 minutes, or until chicken starts to fall off the bones, using 10 coals underneath the oven and 14 on top. Replace coals as needed.

*Boneless, skinless chicken breasts may be substituted, in which case the cooking time may be shorter.

#41

Chicken Pillows

12-INCH DUTCH OVEN • 350 DEGREES • MAKES 8 SERVINGS

2	**boneless, skinless chicken breasts, cut into 1-inch pieces**
2	**bunches green onions, white part only, thinly sliced**
1 package (8 ounces)	**cream cheese, softened**
2 cans (8 ounces each)	**refrigerated crescent roll dough**

Brown and cook chicken pieces thoroughly in Dutch oven, using 20 coals underneath the oven. Remove to a plate and set aside to cool.

In a medium mixing bowl, stir onions into cream cheese until well mixed. Add cooled chicken and stir to combine.

Separate crescent dough into individual triangles. Using a tablespoon, place a scoop of chicken mixture on each piece of dough and roll up, starting with the wide end. There should be enough mixture to fill 16 rolls. Place filled rolls in Dutch oven.* Cover with the lid and bake for 12–15 minutes, or until golden brown, using 10 coals underneath the oven and 14 on top. Remove from oven and serve while still hot.

Variation: If you like gravy, try serving these with chicken or turkey gravy drizzled over top.

*Nonstick cooking spray on the bottom of the Dutch oven can prevent the rolls from sticking. When baked, slide rolls out of the oven with a rubber spatula.

#42

Teriyaki-Barbecue Chicken

14-INCH DUTCH OVEN • 350 DEGREES • MAKES 6–8 SERVINGS

1 bottle (18 ounces)	**teriyaki sauce**
1 bottle (18 ounces)	**barbecue sauce**
6 to 8	**boneless, skinless chicken breasts**
1 can (12 ounces)	**lemon-lime soda**

Pour the teriyaki and barbecue sauces into Dutch oven, stir to combine, and add the chicken. Pour soda evenly over top. Cover with the lid and bake for 30 minutes, or until done, using 12 coals underneath the oven and 16 on top.

#43

Dutch Oven Mutton

12-INCH DUTCH OVEN • 400 DEGREES • MAKES 4–6 SERVINGS

1 to 1½ cups	**olive oil**
4 to 6	**mutton chops, approximately ½ to ¾ inch thick**
1 teaspoon	**seasoned salt**

Pour oil in Dutch oven and heat to almost boiling at 400 degrees using 28 coals underneath. Lay chops on plate, and sprinkle with season salt. Place chops in oil and cook 2 minutes on each side, or until done and fat is crisp.

#44

Chicken Roll-Ups

12-INCH DUTCH OVEN • 350 DEGREES • MAKES 4–6 SERVINGS

1 recipe	**Creamy White Mushroom Sauce (page 80)**
4 to 6 thin slices	**ham**
4 to 6 thin slices	**Asiago cheese**
4 to 6	**boneless, skinless chicken breasts, flattened to 1/4 inch thick**
4 to 6 slices	**peppered bacon, optional**
	salt and pepper, to taste

Prepare the Creamy White Mushroom Sauce and then transfer to the 12-inch oven you will be using for cooking the chicken rolls.

Place 1 slice ham and 1 slice cheese on top of each chicken breast. Starting from the short side, roll up the chicken breast and fillings, tuck in ends, and wrap with 1 slice bacon, if using; secure with toothpicks.

Place chicken rolls in Dutch oven with the mushroom sauce, cover with the lid and bake for 30–40 minutes, or until done, using 10 coals underneath the oven and 14 on top. Season with salt and pepper before serving.

Variation: For bacon lovers, use 2 slices bacon per chicken breast.

#45

Favorite Dutch Oven Lasagna

14-INCH DUTCH OVEN • 350 DEGREES • MAKES 16 SERVINGS

1 package (16 ounces)	**lasagna noodles**
$1\frac{1}{2}$ pounds	**ground beef, cooked and drained**
1	**large onion, chopped**
3 cloves	**garlic, peeled and minced**
2 jars (24 ounces each)	**spaghetti sauce of choice**
1 carton (32 ounces)	**small-curd cottage cheese**
2	**eggs, beaten**
1 package (8 ounces)	**cream cheese, softened**
2 pounds	**shredded mozzarella cheese**

Cook lasagna noodles according to package directions; drain and set aside.

In a large mixing bowl, mix together the beef, onion, and garlic. Add the spaghetti sauce and stir to combine. In a separate bowl, combine the cottage cheese, eggs, and cream cheese.

Layer one-third of the meat mixture, one-third noodles, and one-third cottage cheese mixture in the bottom of Dutch oven. Repeat layers and sprinkle mozzarella cheese evenly over top. Cover with the lid and bake for 45 minutes, or until cheese melts and the sauce is bubbly, using 10 coals underneath the oven and 18 on top.

#46

Stuffed Flank Steak

14-INCH DUTCH OVEN • 350 DEGREES • MAKES 8 SERVINGS

1 (1- to 2-pound)	**flank steak, flattened to 1/4 inch thick**
	salt and pepper, to taste
1/4 cup	**toasted pine nuts**
1/3 cup	**chopped fresh mint**
1/2 cup	**chopped fresh parsley**
5 cloves	**garlic, peeled and crushed**
1/4 cup	**freshly grated Parmesan cheese**
1	**lemon, juiced**
2 tablespoons	**olive oil, divided**
1 to 2 cups	**Fresh Tomato Sauce (page 82)**

Sprinkle both sides of steak with salt and pepper. Place in refrigerator or cooler until ready to use.

In a small bowl, combine nuts, mint, parsley, garlic, cheese, lemon juice, and 1 tablespoon oil; stir together. Remove steak from refrigerator and spread mixture evenly over one side. Roll the steak up across the grain like a jelly roll and tie with kitchen twine to secure at each end and in the middle. Season with more salt and pepper.

In a warmed Dutch oven using 18 to 20 coals underneath the oven, add remaining oil and sear the stuffed steak until browned on all sides. Pour Fresh Tomato Sauce over top, bring to a boil, and remove some of the coals, leaving 10 to 12 underneath the oven. Cover with the lid and place 16 to 18 fresh coals on top. Bring to a simmer and cook for 60 minutes, turning steak a few times during cooking. Replace coals as needed.

Remove steak from oven to a serving platter and let rest for 10–15 minutes. Remove and discard twine and slice steak into 1/2-inch-thick pieces. Serve with warm sauce drizzled over top.

#47

Sweet-and-Sour Dutch Oven

12-INCH DUTCH OVEN • 375–400 DEGREES • MAKES 12 SERVINGS

4 pounds	**beef, pork, or chicken, cut into 1-inch chunks**
4 pounds	**carrots, peeled and sliced**
1 tablespoon	**olive oil**
1 cup	**chopped onion**
4 pounds	**sliced fresh mushrooms**
	water
1 bottle (10 ounces)	**soy sauce**
1 bottle (24 ounces)	**ketchup**
1½ cups	**sugar**
¼ cup	**vinegar**
2 cans (20 ounces each)	**pineapple chunks, drained, juice reserved**
2	**green bell peppers, diced**
	cornstarch
	hot cooked rice, for serving
	sliced green onions, for garnish, optional

Using 20 coals underneath Dutch oven, stir-fry the meat and carrots in oil until meat is cooked through. Add the onion and mushrooms and cook until mushrooms are tender. Add enough water to just cover the bottom of the oven. Add soy sauce, ketchup, sugar, vinegar, and reserved pineapple juice; stir until combined. Bring to a boil and cook, uncovered, for 35–40 minutes, or until the color of the sauce is a burnt orange, using 22 to 30 coals underneath the oven. Replace coals as needed.

Stir in the bell peppers and add enough cornstarch to the sauce to thicken as desired. Remove from heat and stir in pineapple. Serve over hot rice and garnish with green onions, if desired.

#48

Shepherd's Pie

12-INCH DUTCH OVEN • 350 DEGREES • MAKES 12 SERVINGS

2 pounds	**ground beef**
1	**medium onion, chopped**
2 cups	**string beans, peas, or corn (or any combination)**
2 cups	**condensed cream of mushroom soup**
10	**potatoes cooked and mashed***
1 cup	**grated cheddar cheese**

Cook beef and onion in Dutch oven until meat is cooked through, using 12 to 14 coals underneath. Drain grease and then add onion, vegetables, and soup. Spread mashed potatoes over top and sprinkle with cheese. Cover with the lid and bake at 350 degrees using 10 coals underneath and 14 on top for 10 minutes, or until warmed through and cheese is melted.

*4 to 5 cups instant mashed potatoes may be substituted.

#49

Corned Beef Macaroni

12-INCH DUTCH OVEN • 350 DEGREES • MAKES 6–8 SERVINGS

1 can (10.5 ounces)	**condensed cream of mushroom soup**
1 can(10.5 ounces)	**condensed cream of chicken soup**
1 cup	**milk**
1 cup	**grated cheddar cheese**
1 can (12 ounces)	**corned beef**
2 cups	**dry macaroni, cooked and drained**
	salt and pepper, to taste

Mix all ingredients together in Dutch oven, cover with the lid, and bake 30–40 minutes, or until hot and bubbly, at 350 degrees using 10 coals underneath and 14 on top. Season with salt and pepper and stir before serving.

#50

Hamburger Rice Casserole

12-INCH DUTCH OVEN • 350 DEGREES • MAKES 8 SERVINGS

1 pound	**ground beef**
1	**medium onion, chopped**
1 cup	**uncooked white rice**
2 cups	**water**
¼ cup	**soy sauce**
1 can (10.5 ounces)	**condensed cream of mushroom soup**
1 can (10.5 ounces)	**condensed cream of chicken soup**

In Dutch oven, brown beef and onion until meat is cooked through, using 20 to 24 coals underneath. Add rice, water, soy sauce, and soups, cover with the lid, and bake 60–90 minutes at 350 degrees using 10 coals underneath and 14 on top. Check to see if rice is cooked through and stir before serving.

#51

Sausage-Zucchini Rice Casserole

12-INCH DUTCH OVEN • 375 DEGREES • MAKES 8 SERVINGS

2 cups	**uncooked white rice**
1 cup	**chopped celery**
1	**large onion, chopped**
1 pound	**sausage, browned and drained**
4 cubes	**beef bouillon, dissolved in water**
4 cups	**warm water (for the bouillon)**
1 can (10.5 ounces)	**condensed cream of chicken soup**
1 cup	**chopped zucchini**

Layer rice, celery, onion, sausage, bouillon mixture, soup, and zucchini in Dutch oven prepared with nonstick cooking spray. Cover with the lid and bake 60 minutes at 375 degrees using 10 coals underneath and 16 on top. Check to see if rice is cooked through and stir prior to serving.

#52

Easy Chicken and Rice

14-INCH DUTCH OVEN • 350 DEGREES • MAKES 6–8 SERVINGS

2 cups	**uncooked white rice**
2 cans (10.5 ounces each)	**condensed cream of chicken, mushroom, or celery soup**
4 cups	**water**
6	**boneless, skinless chicken breasts**
1 envelope	**dry onion soup mix**
	shredded cheddar cheese, to taste

Stir together the rice, cream soup, and water in Dutch oven until well blended. Place chicken breasts over rice mixture and sprinkle evenly with dry soup mix. Cover with the lid and bake for 60 minutes, or until the rice is cooked and the chicken is done (juices run clear), using 10 coals underneath the oven and 18 on top. Replace coals as needed. Sprinkle cheese over top and let melt before serving.

#53

Chile Verde

12-INCH DUTCH OVEN • 350 DEGREES • MAKES 8 SERVINGS

6	**pork chops, cut into 1-inch pieces**
1/2 pound	**ground beef**
2 tablespoons	**olive oil**
1	**onion, chopped**
1 clove	**garlic, peeled and chopped**
3 cans (4 ounces each)	**chopped green chiles**
2 cans (14.5 ounces each)	**stewed tomatoes, drained**
1	**jalapeño, seeds removed and chopped**
1/2 teaspoon	**salt**
1/8 teaspoon	**freshly ground black pepper**
16	**medium flour tortillas, warmed**
3 cups	**shredded cheddar cheese**

In Dutch oven, brown the pork and beef in oil until meat is cooked through, using 20 coals underneath the oven; drain the grease. Add the onion, garlic, green chiles, tomatoes, jalapeño, salt, and pepper. Cover with the lid and bake for 45–60 minutes, or until meat is tender, using 10 coals underneath the oven and 14 on top, stirring occasionally. Replace coals as needed. Serve over warmed tortillas topped with cheese.

#54

Meat and Cheese–Stuffed Manicotti

10-INCH, 12-INCH DUTCH OVENS • 350 DEGREES • MAKES 4–6 SERVINGS

1 packet (1.37 ounces)	**spaghetti sauce mix**
1 pound	**ground beef**
¼ pound	**shredded Asiago or other sharp cheese**
1 can (8 ounces)	**tomato sauce**
1 package (8 ounces)	**uncooked manicotti shells**
½ pound	**shredded Monterey Jack cheese**

Using 10 coals underneath the 10-inch Dutch oven, make the spaghetti sauce according to package directions and gently simmer.

Brown the ground beef in the 12-inch Dutch oven until cooked through, using 12 to 14 coals underneath the oven; drain grease. Place the cooked beef in a bowl to cool. Once cooled, add the Asiago cheese to beef and stir in the tomato sauce until combined. Gently stuff the manicotti shells with the meat mixture.

Pour enough spaghetti sauce into the bottom of the 12-inch Dutch oven just to cover. Arrange stuffed manicotti over sauce. Spoon any leftover beef mixture over top followed by remaining spaghetti sauce; sprinkle evenly with Monterey Jack cheese. Cover with the lid and bake for 40–45 minutes, or until manicotti shells are soft, using 10 coals underneath the oven and 14 on top. Replace coals as needed.

#55

Apricot and Raspberry-Glazed Cornish Hens

DEEP 14-INCH DUTCH OVEN • 450 DEGREES • MAKES 3–5 SERVINGS

3 to 5	**Cornish hens**
1 can (11.5 ounces)	**apricot nectar**
1 cup	**raspberry vinaigrette**
1 cup	**apricot jam**
1 tablespoon	**all-purpose poultry seasoning**
	salt and pepper, to taste
3 to 10 sprigs	**fresh rosemary**

Rinse hens thoroughly and pat dry with paper towels. Inject apricot nectar into breasts of hens 24 hours before cooking and refrigerate.

In a small bowl, mix the vinaigrette and jam together; set aside.

Preheat Dutch oven to 450 degrees, using 22 coals underneath the oven and 23 on top. Rub the outside of the hens with seasoning and salt and pepper. Place 1 or 2 sprigs of rosemary inside the cavity of each hen. Place hens on a rack in Dutch oven, breast-side up, cover with the lid, and bake for 45–60 minutes. Replace coals as needed.

Remove a few coals to reduce heat as hens begin to brown to prevent burning. Brush hens with half of the jam mixture about 20 minutes before they are finished cooking. Check that the little drumsticks can be easily pulled away from the body of the bird to determine that it is fully cooked. Remove hens to a serving dish and remove and discard the rosemary. Brush remaining jam mixture evenly over each hen just before serving.

#56–61

SIDE DISHES

#56

Cabbage Rolls

12-INCH DUTCH OVEN • 350 DEGREES • MAKES 6 SERVINGS

1½ pounds	**ground beef**
1 large head	**cabbage**
1	**medium onion, finely chopped**
2 tablespoons	**melted butter or oil**
1 cup	**uncooked short grain rice**
¼ cup	**water**
½ teaspoon	**allspice**
	salt and pepper to taste
4 cloves	**garlic, finely chopped and divided**
¼ cup	**lemon juice**

In Dutch oven, brown beef, then drain and set aside. Wipe out Dutch oven with a paper towel. Core cabbage and remove leaves carefully. Boil leaves in salted water until limp and then drain. Wipe Dutch oven dry with paper towel. Fry onion in butter or oil until translucent. Add cooked beef, rice, water, allspice, salt, and pepper. Combine thoroughly.

Place a tablespoon of beef mixture on the bottom edge of a cabbage leaf and roll, tucking sides like an egg roll to contain filling. Place rolls seam-side down and close together in Dutch oven. Sprinkle with garlic and lemon juice. If more than one layer, sprinkle each layer.

Add enough water to just cover rolls. Bring to a simmer using 24 coals underneath. Once simmer is achieved, cover and simmer 60 minutes.

#57

Potatoes, Onion, and Bacon

12-INCH DUTCH OVEN • 350 DEGREES • MAKES 8 SERVINGS

½ to 1 pound	**bacon, cut into 1-inch pieces**
1	**medium onion, sliced**
6 to 8	**red potatoes, sliced**
	salt and pepper, to taste

Cook the bacon in Dutch oven, using 20 to 24 coals underneath the oven. When the bacon is almost cooked, add the onion and continue to cook until the bacon is to your liking. Add the potatoes, salt and pepper, and stir to combine.

Remove the coals you used to cook the bacon. Cover with the lid and bake for 90 minutes, or until potatoes are tender, but not overcooked, using 10 new coals underneath the oven and 14 new coals on top, stirring every 10–15 minutes. Replace coals as needed.

#58

Honey-Glazed Carrots

10-INCH DUTCH OVEN • 325 DEGREES • MAKES 6 SERVINGS

1/4 cup	**butter**
1 pound	**peeled and cut baby carrots**
1/2 cup	**honey**
2 tablespoons	**brown sugar**

Place butter in a warmed* Dutch oven and melt. Add carrots to melted butter, pour honey over top, and sprinkle evenly with brown sugar; stir to coat. Cover with the lid and bake for 30 minutes, or until carrots are fork tender, using 8 coals underneath the oven and 10 on top.

*To warm the Dutch oven, place it in the sun or use 4 coals underneath the oven for a few minutes. You want it warm, not hot.

#59

Corn on the Cob

12-INCH DUTCH OVEN WITH A RACK• 350 DEGREES • MAKES 6 SERVINGS

6 cobs	**fresh sweet corn, still in husks**
½ cup	**water**

Trim ends of corn and husks. Remove outer husk layer, leaving two inner layers. Pull inner layers back slightly to remove silk. Fold husk back over the corn.

Place rack in Dutch oven, add water, and bring to a boil using 30 coals underneath the oven. Layer corn on the rack, cover with the lid, and let steam for 10–20 minutes, or until corn kernels are tender. Remove from Dutch oven and serve immediately.

#60

Cheesy Potatoes

12-INCH DUTCH OVENS • 350 DEGREES • MAKES 12 SERVINGS

6	**large potatoes***
1/4 cup	**butter, melted**
2 cups	**sour cream**
1 can (10.5 ounces)	**condensed cream of chicken soup**
1/4 cup	**chopped onion**
4 cups	**shredded cheddar cheese, divided**

In one of the Dutch ovens, add the potatoes and enough water to completely cover. Cover with the lid and boil the potatoes until fork-tender, using 24 coals underneath the oven and 5 on top. Remove potatoes from oven and set aside to cool. When potatoes have cooled enough to handle, grate them into a large bowl.

Empty the potato water from oven and add the butter, sour cream, soup, and onion. Stir to combine and bring to a simmer for 5 minutes, using the same 24 coals you cooked the potatoes with. Replace coals as needed.

In the second Dutch oven, layer one-third each of the sauce, potatoes, and cheese in that order. Repeat layers until all ingredients are used, finishing with a layer of cheese. Cover with the lid and bake for 20 minutes, or until bubbly and cheese has melted, using 10 coals underneath the oven and 14 on top.

*To save time, skip boiling and grating the potatoes by substituting 1 (2-pound) bag frozen hash brown potatoes that have been thawed.

#61

Dutch Oven Potatoes

12-INCH DUTCH OVEN • 350 DEGREES • MAKES 12–14 SERVINGS

1 pound	**bacon, cut into 1-inch pieces**
10	**medium russet potatoes, peeled and thinly sliced**
5	**carrots, peeled and thinly sliced, optional**
2	**medium onions, diced**
	salt and pepper, to taste
1 can (10.5 ounces)	**condensed cream of mushroom soup**
1 container (24 ounces)	**sour cream**
1 package (8 ounces)	**sliced fresh mushrooms**
1 pound	**shredded cheddar cheese**

In Dutch oven, brown bacon pieces until crisp, using 10 to 12 coals underneath the oven, stirring frequently to prevent burning. Remove bacon and let drain on a paper towel; set aside.

Drain half the grease from the oven and add the potatoes, carrots, if using, and onions. Stir well and add enough water to cover 1 inch in bottom of oven. Season with salt and pepper. Cover with the lid and bake for 35–40 minutes, or until potatoes and carrots are tender, using 10 coals underneath the oven and 14 on top. Replace coals as needed.

In a small bowl, stir soup and sour cream together until smooth. Add soup mixture, mushrooms, and bacon to the potatoes; stir gently to mix. Cover and bake for 10 minutes more. Sprinkle cheese evenly over top and cover until cheese melts.

#62–72

SAUCES, SOUPS & STEWS

#62

Creamy White Mushroom Sauce

10-INCH DUTCH OVEN • 350 DEGREES • MAKES 2 CUPS

1 package (8 ounces)	**sliced fresh mushrooms**
3 tablespoons	**flour**
3 tablespoons	**butter**
1/2 cup	**chicken broth**
1 cup	**light cream or whipping cream**
1/4 cup	**pimientos**
2 teaspoons	**Dijon mustard**

Place mushrooms in large zip-top bag and sprinkle flour over top; seal bag and shake to coat.

Melt butter in Dutch oven, using 10 coals underneath the oven. Add mushrooms and sauté for 5 minutes, or until mushrooms are tender. Add broth and cream and cook until sauce thickens, stirring frequently. Stir in pimientos and mustard.

This is a nice, versatile sauce. Serve over pork chops, use as a base to simmer chicken in, or add some chopped fresh herbs and toss with fettuccine noodles.

#63

Creamy Parmesan Sauce

8-INCH DUTCH OVEN • 300 DEGREES • MAKES 2 CUPS

1 can (10.75 ounces)	**condensed cream of mushroom soup**
1 cup	**milk**
2 tablespoons	**chopped fresh parsley**
1/2 cup	**butter**
3/4 cup	**freshly grated Parmesan cheese**
	salt and pepper, to taste

Place soup, milk, and parsley in Dutch oven; mix until smooth. Add butter and bring mixture to a simmer, using 6 coals underneath the oven. Stir frequently until butter melts and sauce is heated through. Add cheese and stir until completely melted and incorporated into sauce. Season with salt and pepper. Replace coals as needed.

Serve over steamed fresh vegetables, such as broccoli, asparagus, or baby red potatoes. Or stir it into your favorite pasta and add some vegetables and chicken for a nice main dish.

#64

Fresh Tomato Sauce

12-INCH DUTCH OVEN • 350 DEGREES • MAKES 2 CUPS

2 tablespoons	**olive oil**
4 to 8 cloves	**garlic, peeled and crushed**
1/4	**medium onion, finely chopped**
1	**tomato, cored and chopped**
1 can (14 ounces)	**Italian stewed tomatoes, with liquid**
1/4 cup	**chopped fresh parsley**
1 can (14 ounces)	**chicken broth**
1/2 teaspoon	**dried marjoram**
1/2 teaspoon	**dried rosemary, crushed**
1 1/2 tablespoons	**butter**
	salt and pepper, to taste

Heat Dutch oven to 350 degrees using 18 to 20 coals underneath the oven. Add oil, garlic, and onion and sauté until onion is translucent. Add the tomato, stewed tomatoes with liquid, parsley, broth, marjoram, and rosemary; stir to combine. Bring to a boil and then remove enough coals to reduce sauce to a gentle simmer. Cover with the lid and simmer for about 60 minutes, stirring occasionally. Replace coals as needed. Stir in butter and salt and pepper.

This sauce is great served over chicken, pork, or your favorite pasta, or as a pizza sauce, if thickened a bit.

If you would like a thicker sauce, simmer uncovered, stirring occasionally, until sauce has cooked down to desired consistency.

#65

White Chili

12-INCH DUTCH OVEN • 350 DEGREES • MAKES 12–14 SERVINGS

1 pound	**dry white beans**
8 to 10 cups	**water, divided, plus enough to cover beans**
4 tablespoons	**butter**
1	**medium onion, diced**
4 tablespoons	**chicken bouillon granules**
2 teaspoons	**salt, plus more to taste**
2 cans (6.5 ounces each)	**chunk chicken, drained**
2 cans (4 ounces each)	**diced green chiles**
1 container (16 ounces)	**sour cream**
	cilantro, for garnish, optional

Rinse and pick through beans, place in a large bowl, and cover with water; set aside until ready to use.

Melt butter in Dutch oven, using 10 coals underneath the oven. Add onion and sauté until translucent. Drain the beans and add to the onion along with the bouillon, salt, and 8 cups water. Bring to a boil. Cover with the lid and cook for 2–3 hours, or until beans are tender, using 30 to 40 coals underneath the oven, stirring occasionally. Replace coals as needed. Check the water level often and add more if necessary.*

Add the chicken and chiles, replace the lid, and cook for 30 minutes more. Stir in sour cream. Remove enough coals to reduce to a low simmer until ready to serve. Garnish with cilantro before serving, if desired.

*In order to maintain temperature, make sure added water is as hot as possible.

#66

Tortilla Soup

12-INCH DUTCH OVEN • 375 DEGREES • MAKES 15–20 SERVINGS

4 tablespoons	**olive oil, plus extra if needed**
24 (6-inch)	**corn tortillas, cut into 1-inch pieces**
1	**large onion, chopped**
3 cloves	**garlic, peeled and finely chopped**
1	**red bell pepper, seeded and chopped**
4	**yellow wax peppers, seeded and chopped**
4	**boneless, skinless chicken breasts, cut into bite-size chunks**
3 quarts	**water**
2 tablespoons	**pasilla chile powder**
2 tablespoons	**New Mexico chile powder**
2 tablespoons	**California chile powder**
2 cans (16 ounces each)	**diced or stewed tomatoes, with liquid**
1 tablespoon	**salt**
1 pound	**shredded Monterey Jack cheese**
4	**ripe avocados, cut into bite-size chunks, for garnish**

Heat Dutch oven to 375 degrees using 10 to 13 coals underneath the oven. Add enough oil to just cover bottom of oven. Place tortilla pieces, a handful at a time, in hot oil and fry until golden brown. Remove from oil and drain on paper towels; set tortillas chips aside.

Sauté onion, garlic, bell pepper, and yellow peppers in hot oil until onion is translucent. Add chicken and brown until cooked through. Add water, chile powders, tomatoes, and salt; stir. Cover with the lid and simmer for 15 minutes, using the same

13 coals underneath the oven and 16 on top. Replace coals as needed. Just before serving, add the fried tortilla squares to the soup.

To serve, place some cheese in the bottom of individual soup bowls and ladle the hot soup over the cheese. Garnish with avocado chunks.

#67

Good Ol' Dutch Oven Chili

12-INCH DUTCH OVEN • 350 DEGREES • MAKES 10 SERVINGS

1 pound	**ground beef**
1½ cups	**chopped onion**
1½ cups	**chopped green bell pepper**
1 can (29 ounces)	**Italian stewed tomatoes**
1 can (16 ounces)	**tomato sauce**
1 can (15.25 ounces)	**corn, drained**
5 tablespoons	**Worcestershire sauce**
2 teaspoons	**chili powder**
1 teaspoon	**garlic powder**
1 can (32 ounces)	**red beans, rinsed and drained**

In Dutch oven, brown beef, onion, and bell pepper until meat is cooked through, using 30 coals underneath. Add remaining ingredients and remove enough coals from bottom to achieve a simmer. Cover with the lid and let simmer 35–40 minutes, stirring often.

#68

Dutch Oven Stew

12-INCH DUTCH OVEN • 350 DEGREES • MAKES 10–12 SERVINGS

1 pound	**lean beef stew meat**
1	**medium onion, chopped**
2 cans (10.5 ounces each)	**condensed cream of mushroom or chicken soup**
1 to 2 soup cans	**water**
2 cups	**sliced celery**
2 cups	**sliced carrots**
6	**potatoes, cut into cubes**
1 can (14.5 ounces)	**whole kernel corn, with liquid**
1 can (14.5 ounces)	**whole green beans, with liquid**

Place stew meat in Dutch oven, cover with the lid, and brown, using 10 coals underneath the oven and 14 on top. Check often and stir so that the meat is evenly browned on all sides. Add onion, soup, and 1 can water for a thick stew or 2 cans water for a thinner stew. Stir well to combine. Add the celery, carrots, potatoes, corn, and beans.

Bring to a boil using 24 coals underneath the oven, and then remove enough coals to reduce to a low simmer. Cover with the lid and let simmer for 60 minutes, until carrots and potatoes are tender, stirring occasionally. Replace coals as needed.

#69

Kvetcher Stew

12-INCH DUTCH OVEN • 350 DEGREES • MAKES 14–16 SERVINGS

2 pounds	**stew meat, cut in 1-inch cubes**
8	**medium potatoes, quartered**
1 cup	**frozen kernel corn**
4 to 6	**carrots, sliced**
2	**medium onions, coarsely chopped**
4	**medium tomatoes, diced**
2 cloves	**garlic, finely chopped**
1	**green bell pepper, diced**
top 4 inches	**celery stalk, sliced (leaves included)**
3 or 4	**bay leaves**
1 tablespoon	**beef bouillon**
1 cup	**water**

Place stew meat in Dutch oven, cover with the lid, and brown, using 10 coals underneath the oven and 14 on top. Check often and stir so that the meat is evenly browned on all sides. Add remaining ingredients and replace the lid. Check every 20 minutes and stir. Stew is done when potatoes are soft, about 60–90 minutes. Remove bay leaves before serving.

#70

Lamb Stew

12-INCH DUTCH OVEN • 350 DEGREES • MAKES 10–12 SERVINGS

1 to 2 pounds	**fresh lamb**
1 cup	**chopped onion**
2 to 3 cloves	**garlic, chopped**
4 cups	**water**
1 cup	**carrots**
1 can (15.25 ounces)	**whole kernel corn, drained**
1 cup	**chopped celery**
1 cup	**fresh green beans**
2 cups	**cubed potatoes (about 1 inch)**
4 to 8	**beef bouillon cubes***

In a preheated Dutch oven, brown lamb along with onion and garlic. Add the water then add carrots, corn, celery, green beans, and potatoes. Bring to a boil, add bouillon. Remove enough coals to get a good simmer. Simmer the stew for 45–60 minutes at 350 degrees using 10 coals underneath and 14 on top.

*Substitute teaspoons for cubes if using granules.

#71

Chunky Chicken Soup

12-INCH DUTCH OVEN • 350 DEGREES • MAKES 10–12 SERVINGS

1 bottle (24 ounces) ketchup
2 cans (12 ounces each) cola
6 boneless, skinless chicken breasts, cut into 1-inch cubes
6 large russet potatoes, cut into ½-inch cubes
8 large carrots, peeled and cut into ½-inch-thick slices
1 cup uncooked long-grain rice

In Dutch oven, mix together ketchup and cola until well combined. Stir in the chicken, potatoes, carrots, and rice. Cover with the lid and let simmer 60–90 minutes, using 10 coals underneath the oven, stirring occasionally. Replace coals as needed.

This is a thicker soup, so if you prefer a thinner base, gradually add water or chicken broth until desired consistency is reached.

To cook in a shorter amount of time, place 4 to 6 hot coals around the lid, but keep watch to make sure the soup stays at a constant simmer, not a boil.

#72

Hamburger Soup

12-INCH DUTCH OVEN • 350 DEGREES • MAKES 12–16 SERVINGS

1 pound	**ground beef**
1 cup	**chopped onion**
1 cup	**chopped green bell pepper**
1 can (29 ounces)	**Italian stewed tomatoes, with liquid**
1 can (16 ounces)	**tomato sauce**
1 can (15.25 ounces)	**whole kernel corn, drained, optional**
5 tablespoons	**Worcestershire sauce**
2 teaspoons	**chili powder**
1 teaspoon	**garlic powder**
1 can (32 ounces)	**red beans, rinsed and drained**
8 cups	**water**
3	**carrots, peeled and thinly sliced**
3	**russet potatoes, cut into 1-inch cubes**
4 stalks	**celery, sliced**
1	**bay leaf**

Brown beef, onion, and bell pepper in Dutch oven until beef is cooked through, using 30 coals underneath the oven. Drain excess grease and add tomatoes, tomato sauce, corn, if using, Worcestershire sauce, chili powder, garlic powder, beans, water, carrots, potatoes, celery, and bay leaf; stir.

Bring to a boil, and then remove enough coals from underneath the oven to reduce heat to a low simmer. Cover with the lid and simmer for 60 minutes, stirring often. Replace coals as needed. Remove bay leaf before serving.

#73-101

DESSERTS

#73

Raspberry-Peach Pie

12-INCH DUTCH OVEN • 350 DEGREES • MAKES 8 SERVINGS

1½ cups	**sugar**
7 tablespoons	**Clear Jel thickening starch**
6 to 8	**ripe peaches, peeled and sliced**
2 cups	**fresh raspberries**
2 teaspoons	**almond extract**
½ cup	**red wine**
2 cups	**shortening**
4 cups	**flour**
1 cup	**hot water**
½ teaspoon	**salt**
2 tablespoons	**butter, cubed**
¼ cup	**milk**

In a large mixing bowl, mix together the sugar and Clear Jel. Add the fruit, almond extract, and wine. Stir gently.

In a separate bowl, cut shortening into flour with a pastry cutter until it resembles coarse crumbs. Add water and salt and gently toss with a fork just enough to moisten. Knead dough until uniform in texture, and then divide into two balls. On a lightly floured surface, roll one of the dough balls out to a ¼-inch-thick circle, making sure it is large enough to completely cover the bottom of Dutch oven and up the sides about 2 inches. Fold dough in half and gently place in bottom of Dutch oven prepared with nonstick cooking spray or parchment paper.* Unfold dough, and press into the bottom and halfway up the sides of the oven. Carefully spoon the filling over the bottom.

Dot fruit filling with cubes of butter. Roll out second ball of dough for top crust, large enough to cover the filling. Place dough over filling and seal the bottom and top dough edges together with a little bit of water. Cut a few slits for venting. Brush top crust with milk. Cover with the lid and bake for 50–60 minutes, or until the crust turns golden and the filling is bubbling, using 10 coals underneath the oven and 14 to 16 on top. Replace coals as necessary.

*Cut 3 long strips of parchment paper and lay them across each other in a spoke-like pattern in the bottom and up the sides of the oven, pressing firmly in the corners. Cut a round piece of parchment to fit the bottom of the oven and lay it over the strips. The parchment strips will help you lift the pie out of the oven with ease. Make sure the pie is completely cooled before removing from the oven.

#74

Cherry Pie

12-INCH DUTCH OVEN • 400 DEGREES • MAKES 8 SERVINGS

3 cups	**flour**
3½ cups plus 1½ teaspoons	**sugar, divided**
1½ teaspoons	**salt**
¾ teaspoon	**baking powder**
1½ cups	**shortening**
¾ cup	**ice water**
1	**egg**
2 tablespoons	**water**
8 cups	**washed and pitted fresh pie cherries and any excess juice**
2 teaspoons	**Fruit-Fresh Produce Protector**
¾ cup	**Clear Jel thickening starch**
2 teaspoons	**almond extract**

In a large mixing bowl, mix together the flour, 1½ teaspoons sugar, salt, and baking powder. Cut shortening into the flour mixture with a pastry cutter until it resembles coarse crumbs. Slowly stir in the ice water until the mixture holds together and forms a dough. Roll out three-fourths of the dough on a lightly floured surface to a ¼-inch-thick circle, making sure it is large enough to completely cover the bottom of Dutch oven and up the sides about 2 inches. Fold dough in half and gently place in bottom of chilled* Dutch oven prepared with nonstick cooking spray or parchment paper (see tip on page 93). Unfold dough, and press into the bottom and halfway up the sides of the oven.

In a small bowl, whisk together the egg and water, and brush the bottom dough with the egg wash. Place cherries in a large bowl. In a separate bowl, mix 3½ cups sugar, Fruit-Fresh, and Clear Jel together and pour over cherries. Slightly mash the cherries as you stir in the sugar mixture and add the almond extract. Spoon filling into bottom of Dutch oven.

Roll remaining dough out large enough to cover filling; seal the bottom and top dough edges together with water and form a decorative edge, if desired. Cut slits to vent top. Brush with remaining egg wash. Cover with the lid and bake for 60–80 minutes, or until crust turns golden and filling is bubbling, using 12 to 15 coals underneath the oven and 20 on top. Replace coals as necessary.

*To chill the Dutch oven prior to use, set it over a bag of ice.

#75

Pear-Raspberry Pie

12-INCH DUTCH OVEN • 350 DEGREES • MAKES 8 SERVINGS

4 cups	**flour**
2 cups	**shortening**
3/4 teaspoon	**salt, divided**
1 cup	**hot water**
1 cup	**sugar**
3 to 3 1/2 tablespoons	**quick-cooking tapioca**
1/4 teaspoon	**ground nutmeg**
5 to 6	**pears, peeled and sliced**
2 tablespoons	**amaretto**
1 can (21 ounces)	**raspberry pie filling**
1/4 cup	**milk**

In a large mixing bowl, cut flour, shortening, and 1/2 teaspoon salt together with a pastry cutter until crumbly. Add water gradually and gently toss with a fork just enough to moisten. Knead dough until uniform in texture, and then divide into two balls. On a lightly floured surface, roll one of the dough balls out to a 1/4-inch-thick circle. Fold dough in half and place in Dutch oven prepared with nonstick cooking spray or parchment paper (see tip on page 93). It should cover the bottom and just over halfway up the sides of oven.

In a separate bowl, combine sugar, tapioca, remaining 1/4 teaspoon salt, and nutmeg. Add pears and toss to coat. Sprinkle amaretto evenly over coated pears. Place pears in bottom crust, and then spoon pie filling over top. Roll out second dough ball to create top crust and cut slits for venting. Place over filling and seal bottom and top crust edges with water. Brush milk over top. Cover with the lid and bake 50–60 minutes, or until crust is golden brown and filling is bubbling, at 350 degrees using 10 coals underneath and 14 on top.

#76

Pecan Pie

10-INCH DUTCH OVEN • 400 DEGREES • MAKES 8 SERVINGS

4	**eggs**
1⅓ cups	**sugar**
1⅓ cups	**corn syrup***
4 tablespoons	**butter, melted**
1½ teaspoons	**vanilla extract**
1⅓ cups	**chopped pecans**
1 (9-inch)	**refrigerated piecrust**

In a large mixing bowl, beat eggs until well combined; add the sugar and mix well. Stir in the corn syrup. Add butter and vanilla and mix well. Stir in pecans.

Roll the piecrust out so that it is large enough, but not too thin, to press into the bottom and up the sides of Dutch oven prepared with nonstick cooking spray or parchment paper (see tip on page 93). Spoon filling over crust. Cover with the lid and bake for 65–75 minutes, or until a knife inserted into the center comes out with a clear, shiny coating, using 8 coals underneath the oven and 15 on top. Replace coals as needed.

*Light corn syrup gives this pie a lighter taste and color, whereas dark corn syrup will give it a richer taste with a darker color.

#77

Lemonheads Pie

12-INCH DUTCH OVEN • 400 DEGREES • MAKES 8 SERVINGS

6½ cups	**flour, divided**
1⅝ teaspoons	**salt, divided**
1⅔ cups	**shortening**
1¾ cups	**cold water, divided**
3 packages (8 ounces each)	**cream cheese**
2½ cups plus 1 teaspoon	**sugar, divided**
¼ cup	**butter, softened**
6	**eggs**
2	**lemons**
½ cup	**Lemonheads candy, crushed**
1	**egg white, whipped**
½ teaspoon	**cinnamon**

In a large mixing bowl, mix 5 cups flour and 1½ teaspoons salt together. Cut in shortening with a pastry cutter until crumbly. Add 1¼ cups water gradually and mix until dough holds together. Cover and set aside.

In a separate bowl, mix cream cheese, 2½ cups sugar, and butter. Add eggs and mix well, then stir in remaining 1½ cups flour and ⅛ teaspoon salt. Zest 1 lemon and add to cream cheese mixture. Peel and slice remaining lemon paper thin. Add to mixture with remaining ½ cup water. Stir in candy and set aside.

Roll out half the dough, making sure it is large enough to completely cover the bottom of Dutch oven and up the sides about 2 inches. Fold dough in half and gently place in bottom of Dutch oven prepared with parchment paper (see tip on page 93). Unfold dough, and press into the bottom and halfway up the sides of the oven. Pour filling into crust. Roll out remaining dough and place over filling. Seal bottom and top crust edges with water, and cut slits to vent steam. Brush egg white over top, and then sprinkle remaining sugar and cinnamon over top. Cover with the lid and bake 35–45 minutes, or until golden brown, at 400 degrees using 12 coals underneath and 18 on top. Remove from heat, then remove from oven when cooled enough to do so without falling apart. Cool completely on wire rack.

#78

Dump Cobbler

12-INCH DUTCH OVEN • 350 DEGREES • MAKES 12 SERVINGS

1 can (21 ounces)	**apple pie filling**
1 box (15.25 ounces)	**spice cake mix**
1 can	**Dr. Pepper or lemon-lime soda, not diet**

Spoon pie filling in bottom of Dutch oven, then sprinkle cake mix over top. Pour soda over cake mix, trying to completely cover. Cover with the lid and bake at 350 degrees using 10 coals underneath and 14 on top. Bake 30–35 minutes or until cake begins pulling away from sides.

#79

Chocolate Cake

12-INCH CAMP CHEF ULTIMATE DUTCH OVEN • 350 DEGREES • MAKES 12 SERVINGS

Cake:

3 cups	**flour**
1 cup plus 2 tablespoons	**cocoa powder**
3 teaspoons	**baking soda**
¾ teaspoon	**baking powder**
¾ teaspoon	**salt**
1¼ cups	**butter, softened**
3 cups	**sugar**
3	**eggs**
1½ teaspoons	**vanilla extract**
1½ cups	**buttermilk** **(see tip on page 108)**
1 cup plus 2 tablespoons	**sour cream**

Frosting:

1 package (8 ounces)	**cream cheese, softened**
2 tablespoons	**milk**
¼ cup	**sugar**
1 container (12 ounces)	**frozen whipped topping, thawed**
1 box (3.4 ounces)	**instant chocolate pudding mix**

In a large mixing bowl, sift together the flour, cocoa, baking soda, baking powder, and salt; set aside. In a separate bowl, cream the butter and sugar together, and then beat in the eggs and vanilla. Alternately add buttermilk, sour cream, and flour mixture, stirring after each addition. Pour batter into Dutch oven prepared with baking spray. Cover with the lid and bake for 70–80 minutes, or until a toothpick inserted in the center comes out clean, using 9 coals underneath the oven and 16 on top. Replace coals as needed. Let cake cool completely before removing from oven.

For the frosting, mix together the cream cheese, milk, and sugar. Fold in whipped topping and pudding mix until thoroughly combined. Frost the cake when cooled.

#80

Southern-Style Peach Cobbler

12-INCH DUTCH OVEN • 350 DEGREES • MAKES 12 SERVINGS

2 cups	**flour**
2 cups	**sugar**
2 cups	**evaporated milk**
1 cup	**butter, melted**
2 cans (29 ounces each)	**peaches, juice reserved**

In a bowl, combine flour, sugar, evaporated milk, butter, and ½ cup reserved peach juice until smooth. Place peaches in the bottom of Dutch oven prepared with nonstick cooking spray. Pour batter over top. Cover with the lid and bake at 350 degrees using 10 coals underneath and 14 on top. Bake 30–35 minutes, or until golden brown. Serve warm.

#81

Raspberry-Peach Cobbler

12-INCH DUTCH OVEN • 350 DEGREES • MAKES 12 SERVINGS

1 can (29 ounces) **peach slices or halves**
1 can (21 ounces) **raspberry pie filling, divided**
1 box (15.25 ounces) **yellow cake mix**
ice cream, for serving, optional

Drain juice from peaches and set aside. Place peach slices in the bottom of Dutch oven, reserving three to four slices. Cut reserved slices into small pieces and place in a small bowl; stir in 4 teaspoons pie filling and set aside. Spoon remaining pie filling over peaches in bottom of oven.

In a large mixing bowl, make cake batter according to package directions, eliminating the eggs and using the reserved peach juice in place of water. If there isn't enough juice, add water to make up the difference. Stir the reserved peach and pie filling mixture into the batter and then evenly pour batter over the fruit in the bottom of the oven. Cover with the lid and bake for 30–35 minutes, or until the cake begins to pull away from the sides, using 10 coals underneath the oven and 14 on top. Serve warm and topped with ice cream, if desired.

#82

Banana Cake

12-INCH DUTCH OVEN • 350 DEGREES • MAKES 12 SERVINGS

⅔ cup	**sugar**
⅓ cup	**shortening**
2	**eggs**
3 tablespoons	**buttermilk***
4 to 5	**overripe bananas, mashed**
2 cups	**flour**
½ teaspoon	**baking soda**
1 teaspoon	**baking powder**
½ teaspoon	**salt**
½ cup	**chocolate chips**

In a large mixing bowl, cream the sugar and shortening together. Add the eggs, buttermilk, and bananas; stir well to combine. Mix in the flour, baking soda, baking powder, and salt until well blended and smooth. Add chocolate chips. Pour batter into Dutch oven prepared with baking spray. Cover with the lid and bake for 35–40 minutes, or until a toothpick inserted in the center comes out clean, using 10 coals underneath the oven and 14 on top.

*Make your own buttermilk by combining 3 tablespoons milk with 1 teaspoon lemon juice.

#83

Chocolate-Peppermint Cake

12-INCH DUTCH OVEN • 350 DEGREES • MAKES 12 SERVINGS

Cake:

3 cups	**sifted flour**
1 teaspoon	**salt**
2 teaspoons	**baking soda**
4 heaping tablespoons	**cocoa**
2 cups	**sugar**
2 teaspoons	**vinegar**
10 tablespoons	**butter, melted**
1/4 teaspoon	**peppermint extract**
2 cups	**cold water**
3/4 cup	**semisweet chocolate chips**

Frosting:

1/4 teaspoon	**salt**
1/4 cup	**sugar**
2	**egg whites, beaten**
3/4 cup	**light corn syrup**
1 1/2 tablespoons	**vanilla extract**
1/8 cup	**crushed peppermint candies**
1/8 cup	**chocolate syrup**

In a large mixing bowl, sift together the flour, salt, baking soda, cocoa, and sugar; set aside. In a separate bowl, combine the vinegar, butter, peppermint extract, and water; mix well. Add to dry ingredients and stir until smooth; stir in chocolate chips. Pour batter into Dutch oven prepared with baking spray. Cover with the lid and bake for 30 minutes, or until a toothpick inserted in the center comes out clean, using 10 coals underneath the oven and 14 on top. Let cake cool before removing from Dutch oven.

For the frosting, in a medium mixing bowl, gradually add salt and sugar to egg whites, beating until smooth. Slowly add corn syrup and beat until stiff peaks form; gently fold in the vanilla. Frost cooled cake and sprinkle candies over top. Drizzle chocolate syrup over individual servings.

#84

Devil's Food Cake

12-INCH DUTCH OVEN • 350 DEGREES • MAKES 12 SERVINGS

2 boxes (15.25 ounces each)	**devil's food cake mix**
1 package (12 ounces)	**mini mint chips**
1 can (21 ounces)	**cherry pie filling**

In a large mixing bowl, cake batter according to package directions. Fold in mint chips. Pour into Dutch oven prepared with baking spray. Cover with the lid and bake at 350 degrees using 10 coals underneath and 14 on top. Bake 15–18 minutes, and then remove coals from bottom of oven. Place 8 more coals on top 45 minutes more, or until toothpick inserted in center comes out clean. Remove cake from Dutch oven and place on wire rack. When cake is completely cool, spoon pie filling over top.

#85

Apple Spice Cake

12-INCH, 10-INCH DUTCH OVENS • 375 DEGREES • MAKES 12 SERVINGS

Cake:

1 box (15.25 ounces)	**spice cake mix**
1¼ cups	**water**
⅓ cup	**vegetable oil**
3	**egg whites**
2 cans (21 ounces each)	**apple pie filling**

Sauce:

1½ cups	**light brown sugar**
¾ cup	**light corn syrup**
4 tablespoons	**butter**
½ cup	**light cream**

In a large mixing bowl, combine cake mix, water, oil, and egg whites until thoroughly mixed; set aside.

Fit a piece of parchment paper in the bottom of 12-inch Dutch oven. Pour pie filling over parchment paper and then pour the batter over pie filling.

Cover with the lid and bake for 25–35 minutes, or until a toothpick inserted in the center comes out clean, using 8 coals underneath the oven and 18 on top. Remove from Dutch oven by gently jiggling cake to loosen from the sides of the oven. Invert cake onto a cool, 12-inch Dutch oven lid and remove parchment paper.

For the sauce, in 10-inch Dutch oven, heat the brown sugar, corn syrup, and butter over a low heat until mixture reaches a soft-ball stage, stirring occasionally, using 10 coals underneath the oven. Add the cream and heat for 2 minutes more. Serve cake with sauce drizzled over top.

#86

Lemon-Orange Cake

12-INCH DUTCH OVEN • 350 DEGREES • MAKES 12 SERVINGS

Cake:

1 box (15.25 ounces)	**lemon cake mix**
1 box (3.4 ounces)	**vanilla instant pudding mix**
4	**eggs**
½ cup	**vegetable oil**
1 cup	**water**

Glaze:

2 teaspoons	**butter, melted**
½ cup	**orange juice**
1	**orange zested, for garnish, optional**

In a large mixing bowl, combine cake mix, pudding mix, eggs, oil, and water; blend well. Pour batter into Dutch oven prepared with baking spray. Cover with the lid and bake for 30–35 minutes, or until a toothpick inserted in the center comes out clean, using 10 coals underneath the oven and 14 on top. Let cake cool completely before removing from oven.

For the glaze, in a separate bowl, mix butter, orange juice, and powdered sugar together until smooth. If glaze is too runny, add more powdered sugar until desired consistency is achieved. Poke holes in the top of cooled cake using the handle of a wooden spoon and pour glaze over top. Garnish with orange zest, if desired. Let rest 10–15 minutes before serving.

#87

Carrot Cake

14-INCH DUTCH OVEN • 350 DEGREES • MAKES 16 SERVINGS

2 cups	**flour**
2 teaspoons	**baking soda**
1 teaspoon	**nutmeg**
2 teaspoons	**cinnamon**
½ teaspoon	**salt**
3	**eggs, beaten**
¾ cup	**vegetable oil**
¾ cup	**buttermilk***
2 cups	**sugar**
2 teaspoons	**vanilla extract**
1 can (8 ounces)	**crushed pineapple, drained**
2 cups	**grated carrots**
1½ cups	**coconut**
½ cup	**raisins**
1 cup	**chopped pecans**
1 container (16 ounces)	**cream cheese frosting**

Sift together flour, baking soda, nutmeg, cinnamon, and salt and set aside. In a large mixing bowl, beat eggs, oil, buttermilk, sugar, and vanilla. Add sifted dry ingredients, pineapple, carrots, coconut, raisins, and pecans. Pour batter into Dutch oven prepared with nonstick spray containing flour. Cover with the lid and bake at 350 degrees using 11 coals underneath and 17 on top. Bake 55–65 minutes, or until toothpick inserted in center comes out clean. Remove from Dutch oven and place on wire rack until completely cool, and then frost.

*Make your own buttermilk by combining ¾ cup milk and 4 teaspoons lemon juice.

#88

Zucchini-Carrot Cake

12-INCH CAMP CHEF ULTIMATE DUTCH OVEN • 350 DEGREES • MAKES 12 SERVINGS

Cake:

½ cup	**oil**
2 cups	**sugar**
3	**eggs**
3 teaspoons	**vanilla**
2 cups	**shredded zucchini**
1 cup	**shredded carrots**
1 can (8 ounces)	**crushed pineapple, with liquid**
1 teaspoon	**salt**
1 tablespoon	**cinnamon**
¼ teaspoon	**baking powder**
1 teaspoon	**baking soda**
3 cups	**flour**
½ cup	**chopped walnuts**

Frosting:

1 package (8 ounces)	**cream cheese, softened**
½ cup	**butter, softened**
1 teaspoon	**vanilla**
4 cups	**powdered sugar**

In a large mixing bowl, cream oil, sugar, eggs, and vanilla. Stir in zucchini and carrots, then add pineapple and mix well. Add salt, cinnamon, baking powder, baking soda, and flour. Fold in nuts. Pour batter into Dutch oven prepared with nonstick spray containing flour. Cover with the lid and bake at 350 degrees using 10 coals underneath and 14 on top. Bake 40–50 minutes, or until toothpick inserted in center comes out clean.

For the frosting, combine cream cheese and butter in a bowl until smooth. Stir in vanilla, and then add powdered sugar 1 cup at a time until well blended. Frost cooled cake and serve.

#89

Pumpkin Spice Cake

10-INCH DUTCH OVEN • 350 DEGREES • MAKES 10 SERVINGS

Cake:

2 cups	**flour**
1 1/3 cups	**sugar**
1 1/4 teaspoons	**baking powder**
3/4 teaspoon	**salt**
2 teaspoons	**pumpkin pie spice**
1/4 teaspoon	**baking soda**
1 1/4 cups	**pumpkin (not pumpkin pie filling)**
1 cup	**evaporated milk**
3	**eggs**
1 teaspoon	**vanilla**
1/3 cups	**oil**

Frosting:

4 ounces	**cream cheese, softened**
1/4 cup	**butter, softened**
2 tablespoons	**sour cream**
2 tablespoons	**orange juice**
1/2 teaspoon	**vanilla**
2 1/2 cups	**powdered sugar**
	orange food coloring

In a bowl, combine flour, sugar, baking powder, salt, pumpkin pie spice, and baking soda and set aside.

In a separate bowl, combine pumpkin, milk, eggs, vanilla, and oil. Combine with dry ingredients until well blended. Pour batter into Dutch oven prepared with nonstick spray containing flour. Cover with the lid and bake 35–40 minutes or until done, at 350 degrees using 8 coals underneath and 13 on top.

For the frosting, beat together cream cheese and butter in a bowl. Add sour cream, orange juice, and vanilla. Add powdered sugar gradually until blended and smooth. Stir in a couple drops orange food coloring. Frost cooled cake and serve.

#90

Oatmeal Cobbler

12-INCH DUTCH OVEN • 350 DEGREES • MAKES 12 SERVINGS

1 box (15.25 ounces)	**yellow cake mix**
½ cup	**butter**
2 cups	**quick oats**
1 can (21 ounces)	**cherry pie filling**
	vanilla ice cream

In a bowl, combine cake mix, butter, and oats until crumbly and set aside. Spoon pie filling in Dutch oven prepared with nonstick cooking spray. Sprinkle crumb mixture over top. Cover with the lid and bake at 350 degrees using 10 coals underneath and 14 on top. Bake 30 minutes, or until filling is bubbling through top. Serve warm with vanilla ice cream.

Variation: Any flavor of fruit pie filling may be used.

#91

Pumpkin Crumble

12-INCH DUTCH OVEN • 325 DEGREES • MAKES 12 SERVINGS

Cake:

1 cup	**sugar**
1½ teaspoons	**cinnamon**
½ teaspoon	**ginger**
½ teaspoon	**ground cloves**
1 can (12 ounces)	**evaporated milk**
½ teaspoon	**salt**
½ teaspoon	**nutmeg**
½ teaspoon	**allspice**
1½ cups	**pumpkin (not pumpkin pie filling)**
2	**eggs**

Topping:

½ cup	**butter, softened**
1½ cups	**sugar**
2¼ cups	**flour**
2½ teaspoons	**baking powder**
1 teaspoon	**salt**

In a large mixing bowl, mix all the cake ingredients together until smooth. Pour batter into Dutch oven prepared with nonstick cooking spray.

In a separate bowl, combine butter, sugar, flour, baking powder, and salt until crumbly. Sprinkle over batter. Cover with the lid and bake at 325 degrees using 8 coals underneath and 16 on top. Bake 30–35 minutes, or until toothpick inserted in center comes out clean. After 30 minutes of baking, remove 3 coals from bottom and move to top so bottom of cake doesn't burn.

#92

Apple Crunch

12-INCH DUTCH OVEN • 350 DEGREES • MAKES 12 SERVINGS

15 to 16	**apples, peeled and sliced**
1 cup	**sugar**
1 cup	**water**
1 tablespoon	**vanilla**
1 tablespoon	**cornstarch**

Topping:

1 cup	**flour**
3/4 cup	**quick oats**
1 cup	**brown sugar**
2 teaspoons	**cinnamon**
1/2 cup	**butter, softened**

Place apples in Dutch oven prepared with nonstick cooking spray. In a saucepan, heat sugar, water, vanilla, and cornstarch until thickened. Pour evenly over apples.

In a bowl, combine topping flour, oats, brown sugar, cinnamon, and butter and then sprinkle over apples. Cover with the lid and bake at 350 degrees using 10 coals underneath and 14 on top. Bake 60 minutes, or until apples are tender. Allow to cool 15–20 minutes before serving.

#93

Apple Cinnamon Cake

12-INCH DUTCH OVEN • 350 DEGREES • MAKES 12 SERVINGS

2	**eggs**
½ teaspoon plus 1 pinch	**salt**
1½ cups	**sugar**
2¾ teaspoons	**vanilla extract, divided**
1 cup	**vegetable oil**
2 tablespoons	**lemon juice**
1 tablespoon	**lemon zest**
3 heaping cups	**flour**
1¾ teaspoons	**cinnamon, divided**
1¼ teaspoons	**baking soda**
¼ teaspoon	**nutmeg**
3 to 4	**Granny Smith apples, peeled, cored, and grated (about 3 cups)**
1 package (8 ounces)	**cream cheese, softened**
¾ cup	**butter**
4 cups	**powdered sugar**
	sliced almonds, for garnish

In a large mixing bowl, beat together eggs, ½ teaspoon salt, sugar, 2 teaspoons vanilla, oil, lemon juice, and lemon zest and set aside.

In a separate bowl, combine flour, 1 teaspoon cinnamon, baking soda, and nutmeg. Gradually mix into the egg mixture and then stir in apples.

Pour batter into Dutch oven prepared with baking spray. Cover with the lid and bake at 350 degrees using 10 coals underneath and 14 on top. Bake 75 minutes, or until toothpick inserted in center comes out clear. Remove cake from Dutch oven and cool.

In a bowl, combine remaining pinch salt, 1 3/4 teaspoons vanilla, 3/4 teaspoon cinnamon, cream cheese, and butter. Add powdered sugar 1 cup at a time and beat until smooth. Frost cooled cake and sprinkle almonds over top.

#94

Caramel Apple Cobbler

14-INCH DUTCH OVEN • 350 DEGREES • MAKES 16 SERVINGS

4 cans (21 ounces each)	**apple pie filling**
2 boxes (32 ounces each)	**Krusteaz cinnamon crumb cake mix**
1 jar (20 ounces)	**caramel ice cream topping**
	vanilla ice cream

Spoon pie filling into bottom of Dutch oven. Mix cake batter according to package directions. Pour batter over pie filling. Cover with the lid and bake at 350 degrees using 10 coals underneath and 18 on top. Bake 30–35 minutes, or until toothpick inserted in center comes out clean. When cake is done, remove coals from bottom and place on top 3–5 minutes more to make top slightly crusty. Remove from heat. Pour caramel over top and serve with a scoop of vanilla ice cream.

#95

White Chocolate Cheesecake

10-INCH DUTCH OVEN • 325 DEGREES • MAKES 12 SERVINGS

7	**whole graham crackers**
1/4 cup	**butter, cubed and softened**
1 cup	**low-fat sour cream**
4	**eggs, separated into yolks and whites**
1/2 cup	**sugar**
1 tablespoon	**cornstarch**
3 packages (8 ounces each)	**low-fat cream cheese, softened**
5 ounces	**white baking chocolate, melted**
2 tablespoons	**lemon juice**
2 tablespoons	**vanilla extract**
2 tablespoons	**hot fudge ice cream topping**
2 tablespoons	**caramel ice cream topping**
1/2 cup	**chopped pecans**
1/3 cup	**semisweet chocolate chips**

Place graham crackers in a large zip-top bag, and crush to fine crumbs with a rolling pin. Add butter, seal bag, and mash together with your hands. Press crust mixture in the bottom and partway up the sides of Dutch oven lined with parchment paper (see tip on page 93).

In a large mixing bowl, blend together the sour cream, egg yolks, sugar, cornstarch, cream cheese, white chocolate, lemon juice, and vanilla.

In a separate bowl, beat egg whites until stiff peaks form. Fold egg whites into cheesecake filling until combined. Pour filling over crust. Cover with the lid and bake for 45–60 minutes, or until center jiggles when lightly shaken, using 8 coals underneath the oven and 11 coals on top. Replace coals as needed. Remove from heat and let cool for 60 minutes. Carefully remove from oven with liner. Garnish with hot fudge, caramel, pecans, and chocolate chips.

#96

Peachy Dump Cake

12-INCH DUTCH OVEN • 350 DEGREES • MAKES 12 SERVINGS

2 cans (19 ounces each)	**peaches, drained**
2 boxes (15.25 ounces each)	**white cake mix**
2 cans (12 ounces each)	**lemon-lime soda, not diet**
1 package (8 ounces)	**Red Hot candies**

Place peaches evenly underneath of Dutch oven. Sprinkle cake mix evenly over top. Pour soda over cake mix, trying to completely cover. Sprinkle candies over top. Cover with the lid and bake at 350 degrees using 10 coals underneath and 14 on top. Bake 45–50 minutes, or until cake pulls away from sides of oven.

#97

Strawberry Torte

10-INCH DUTCH OVEN • 350 DEGREES • MAKES 10 SERVINGS

Cake:

2 cups	**flour**
1/2 cup	**vegetable oil**
1 1/3 cups	**sugar**
1 cup	**milk**
1 1/4 teaspoons	**baking powder**
1 teaspoon	**vanilla extract**
3/4 teaspoon	**salt**
2	**eggs**

Filling:

1 3/4 cups	**milk**
1 package (8 ounces)	**cream cheese**
1 box (3.4 ounces)	**instant vanilla pudding mix**
1 teaspoon	**lemon zest**

Glaze:

2 cups	**water**
4 tablespoons	**cornstarch**
1 envelope	**strawberry Kool-Aid**
1 cup	**sugar**
1 quart	**fresh strawberries, hulled and sliced**

In a large mixing bowl, add flour, vegetable oil, sugar, milk, baking powder, vanilla, salt, and eggs, and mix until well combined. Pour into Dutch oven prepared with baking spray. Cover with the lid and bake for 30–35 minutes, or until a toothpick inserted in the center comes out clean, using 8 coals underneath the oven and 12 on top. Remove from heat and let cake cool completely before removing it from the oven.

For the filling, in a separate bowl, add ½ cup milk at a time to cream cheese, beating together until blended. Beat in pudding mix and lemon zest; refrigerate or place in a cooler until ready to use.

For the glaze, in a medium saucepan over 3 to 4 coals, bring the water, cornstarch, Kool-Aid, and sugar to a boil, stirring constantly, until thickened. Remove from heat and place in a bowl to cool. Cover with a lid or plastic wrap to prevent a skin from forming.

Using a paring knife, score a line around the outside of the cooled cake to use as a cutting guide. Cut horizontally through the center of the cake to make 2 layers using a serrated knife, or by sliding a string into the scored guide and pulling it through the cake.

Set the top half aside and spread a thin layer of glaze over the bottom half. Spread half the filling over the glaze and arrange half the strawberries evenly over top. Replace the top half of cake and spread remaining glaze in a 7-inch circle on top of cake. Use remaining filling to frame glaze, and place remaining strawberries on top.

#98

Smacos

12-INCH DUTCH OVEN • 350 DEGREES • MAKES 10 SERVINGS

1 teaspoon	**olive oil**
10	**medium flour tortillas**
$1\frac{1}{2}$ cups	**semisweet chocolate chips, divided in 10 equal groups**
1 package (16 ounces)	**mini marshmallows, divided in 10 equal groups**

Using a paper towel, spread oil over bottom of Dutch oven. Heat Dutch oven using 10 to 14 coals underneath.

Place a tortilla in bottom of heated oven and layer one group chocolate chips and then one group marshmallows over top. Cover with lid for 1 minute. Remove lid and using a pair of tongs fold the tortilla in half, making a taco shape. Cover for another minute. Remove lid and then use tongs to place on a paper plate and cool. Repeat with remaining ingredients. Serve when cooled enough to handle.

#99

Snack Cake

14-INCH DUTCH OVEN • 350 DEGREES • MAKES 16 SERVINGS

1 can (29 ounces)	**pears, with juice**
4 cups	**flour**
2 cups	**sugar**
4 teaspoons	**baking soda**
1 teaspoon	**salt**
4 teaspoons	**cinnamon**
1 teaspoon	**nutmeg**
½ teaspoon	**ground cloves**
1 cup	**oil**
2 cups	**brown sugar**
2 cups	**chocolate chips**

Mash pears in their juice and set aside.

In a large bowl, combine flour, sugar, baking soda, salt, cinnamon, nutmeg, ground cloves, and oil. Add mashed pears to mixture. Pour into Dutch oven prepared with nonstick cooking spray. Sprinkle brown sugar and chocolate chips over top. Cover with the lid and bake at 350 degrees using 10 coals underneath and 18 on top. Bake 25 minutes, or until a toothpick inserted in the center comes out clean.

#100

S'mores Brownies

12-INCH DUTCH OVEN • 400 DEGREES • MAKES 12 SERVINGS

1 cup	**butter, melted**
½ cup	**cocoa**
4	**eggs**
2 cups	**sugar**
1 teaspoon	**vanilla**
1 teaspoon	**cinnamon**
½ teaspoon	**salt**
½ teaspoon	**baking powder**
2 cups	**flour**
¾ cup	**chopped pecans**
1 cup	**mini marshmallows**
1 cup	**chopped peanut butter cups**

In a mixing bowl, whisk butter and cocoa together. Add eggs one at a time, whisking between each. Add sugar, vanilla, cinnamon, salt, baking powder, and flour. Pour into Dutch oven prepared with baking spray. Sprinkle pecans over top. Cover with the lid and bake at 400 degrees using 18 coals underneath and 12 on top. Bake 12 minutes, and then remove heat from bottom, but continue baking with top heat 15–20 minutes more. Remove lid and sprinkle with marshmallows and peanut butter cups. Replace lid and remove all coals. Let sit 5–10 minutes before serving.

#101

Sweet Poached Pears

12-INCH DUTCH OVEN • 350 DEGREES • MAKES 6 SERVINGS

1 tablespoon	**butter**
1/4 cup	**ginger ale, not diet**
25	**caramels, unwrapped**
25	**cinnamon candies, such as Hot Tamales or Red Hots**
1 box (8 ounces)	**Red Hots candies**
6	**ripe but firm pears, peeled**

Heat the butter, ginger ale, caramels, and candies in a warmed* Dutch oven, with 10 coals underneath, until caramels and candies have melted, stirring occasionally. Add more ginger ale as needed to cover the bottom of oven with poaching liquid 1/4 inch deep.

Place pears in Dutch oven standing up. If pears are having a problem standing, slice a piece off the bottoms to make them more level. Cover with the lid and bake until fork-tender, using 10 coals underneath the oven and 13 on top. Baste pears with cooking sauce occasionally while they are cooking. When done, carefully remove pears and place on a cool serving platter. Drizzle cooking sauce over pears to serve.

*To warm the Dutch oven, place it in the sun or use 4 coals underneath the oven for a few minutes. You want it warm, not hot.

NOTES

NOTES

NOTES

Metric Conversion Chart

VOLUME MEASUREMENTS

U.S.	Metric
1 teaspoon	5 ml
1 tablespoon	15 ml
¼ cup	60 ml
⅓ cup	75 ml
½ cup	125 ml
⅔ cup	150 ml
¾ cup	175 ml
1 cup	250 ml

WEIGHT MEASUREMENTS

U.S.	Metric
½ ounce	15 g
1 ounce	30 g
3 ounces	90 g
4 ounces	115 g
8 ounces	225 g
12 ounces	350 g
1 pound	450 g
2¼ pounds	1 kg

TEMPERATURE CONVERSION

Fahrenheit	Celsius
250	120
300	150
325	160
350	180
375	190
400	200
425	220
450	230

About the Author

Vernon Winterton has been cooking in Dutch ovens for over forty years. He is one of the founding members of the Greater Wasatch Dutch Oven Society and served two years as its assistant director. Vernon has competed in numerous Dutch oven cook-offs over the years, qualifying three times to go to the world championships. He lives in Lehi, Utah.